Secrets

of the

Miniature Rose

ELIZABETH ABLER

TAYLOR TRADE PUBLISHING

Lanham   New York   Oxford

DISCARDED
From the Nashville Public Library

First Taylor Trade Publishing edition 2003

This Taylor Trade Publishing edition of *Secrets of the Miniature Rose* is an original publication. It is published with arrangement with the editor.

Copyright © 2003 by Elizabeth Abler

All rights reserved.
No part of this book may be reproduced in any form or by any electronic or mechanical means, including information storage and retrieval systems, without written permission.

Published by Taylor Trade Publishing
A Member of the Rowman & Littlefield Publishing Group
4501 Forbes Boulevard, Suite 200
Lanham, Maryland 20706

Distributed by National Book Network

Library of Congress Cataloging-in-Publication Data
Abler, Elizabeth.
  Secrets of the miniature rose / Elizabeth Abler.
    p.   cm.
  Includes bibliographical references and index.

  1. Miniature roses. I. Title.
  SB411.65.M55 A35 2003
  635.9'33734—dc21

                          2003000818

  ISBN: 978-0-87833-311-0

∞ The paper used in this publication meets the minimum requirements of American National Standard for Information Sciences—Permanence of Paper for Printed Library Materials, ANSI/NISO Z39.48–1992.

Manufactured in the United States of America.

Would Love a
Queen of Flowers ordain
The Rose, the
Queen of Flowers,
Should reign

SAPPHO
(c. 610–580 B.C.)

CONTENTS

❧

Contents

PREFACE

✣

ROSES ARE the music of flowerdom. Although poets and artists throughout the centuries have given us their eloquence and talent, there's no describing the appeal of a beautiful rose. Miniature roses are the latest and newest style of rose to have achieved a warm place in the hearts and lives of man.

This book is intended to explore the ways in which miniature roses can be a part of everyone's living, to demonstrate how simply and easily they may be cared for, the varied ways they may be enjoyed. Reading this book for information and using it as a guide should help the reader feel at home and comfortable in handling miniroses, whether two or two hundred are involved.

Since all rose activities are inter-related, it's best to read, or at least scan the entire book before bearing down on any one section. The Miniature Directions following each chapter synopsize the chapter's main ideas and serve as reminder and reference.

—ELIZABETH ABLER

Secrets

of the

Miniature Rose

CHAPTER 1

A Short History

NOW THAT miniature roses are sold by the millions in the United States and around the world, and every year you read illustrated catalogues offering them, and they are the pet and occasionally the exacerbation of rosarians, it may be difficult to imagine that they were new and exciting and popular more than a hundred and fifty years ago. Only then they were called fairy roses, especially in England, and are still so known to some extent.

Roses have existed in this country for millions of years, as fossils found in Colorado bear witness, but in miniature form are a relatively new phenomenon.

Prior to their arrival in the west, miniatures were known only in China where, it is thought, generations of gardeners saved seed from bushes with the smallest flowers, planted these and painstakingly strived toward their goal of truly minute roses to please the nobility and royalty whom they served. On the other hand, since we know evolution's dependency, we conclude that there were contributions from mutations as well. Because miniature roses never have been found in the wild in China, or anywhere else, it must be that sedulous gardeners labored through long centuries to achieve what we now so happily enjoy.

There is no need to look below the equator because no roses have ever evolved there. The many beautiful roses below the equator are descendants of immigrants.

Though much of minirose history is clouded in confusion and myth, certain facts do anchor the tales. With trade in horticulture fundamental to the growth and commerce of nations, in due course minirose cuttings reached the island of Mauritius and were awaiting British occupation there.

In 1818, English botanist Robert Sweet listed for sale a miniature rose, which he called *R. Lawrenceana*, as coming from Mauritius in 1810. Curtis's *Botanical Magazine* of 1815 contains a plate and description of *R. semperflorens minima*, or Miss Lawrence's rose, named in tribute to the quite well known and admired painter, Mary Lawrence, who chose roses as the subject of her book of colored plates. Published in 1799, her work created a sensation because no such book had been known before, and roses were appearing in increasing numbers in English gardens. A new kind of rose named after such a person could only thrive. The miniature rose was on its way.

It is believed that the first miniatures had five petals, like the wild roses in the fossil record, but when many-petaled forms appeared, speculation arose that these might have been the original—characteristic of some of the uncertain history of rose origins. Interest grew, but not until 1894 was the minirose given its rightful name, *R. chinensis minima*.

Markets in England, then America, France, and other countries of Europe catered to the demand for novelty roses. When they appeared in France, the aristocracy lionized the miniatures for their petiteness and color, using them as show pieces both indoors and out. Minirose popularity was such that they were clustered on windowsills as exciting conversation pieces. In fact, they were advertised as "pour l'ornement des fenêtres."

M'Intosh, Belgian royal gardener, in his *Flower Garden*, published in 1829, mentions the usual Gloire de Laurence, but also Petite Laponne, crimson, and La Miniature, pink. Elsewhere we get reports that these rosebushes were no larger than a teacup. By the time they were advertised in botanical magazines and catalogues, they were being sold in the thousands. Varieties, forgotten today, were shades of red and pink, from pale to bright, and white. Jenny was a bright crimson; Nigra, very dark.

William Paul, in the 1863 edition of his *Rose Garden*, lists seven other varieties: La Désirée, Nemesis, Alba, Retour du Printemps, Fairy, Red Pet, Gloire des Laurenceanas.

In the United States miniature roses were popular during the 1840s and for a time thereafter, but dropped from sight during the next generation. About thirty varieties had been offered to the public by commercial importers before they disappeared completely from the marketplace. Polyanthas, also small of flower but large of bush, caused fairy roses to lose out; plus, as, of course, did tea roses and particularly the hybrid perpetual American Beauty, which became the rage. All suitable, perhaps, to layers of petticoats, bustles, and voluminous skirts. Even today the name American Beauty evokes visions of large red hybrid teas, although technically an American Beauty is a deep pink hybrid perpetual.

Fairy roses, indeed, because this can be called a fairy tale for gardeners. Miniature roses, now off the market and forgotten by the public in both Europe and America, were due for a remarkable comeback. Waiting in the wings, so to speak.

In 1919 a Swiss army surgeon, Dr. Roulet, found some miniature roses, which he called midgets, growing in pots on the windowsills of cottages at Mauborjet in the Jura Mountains. Intrigued by their size, Colonel Roulet offered cuttings to his friend Henri Correvon, a plant and rock garden authority. From these M. Correvon propagated a sufficient number of plants to offer them for sale at the Paris flower market, calling his product Rosa Rouletti, for Colonel Roulet. M. Correvon held the opinion that the tiny rose was better grown in a pot on a windowsill than outdoors in the ground, for that way it retained its miniature character, he believed.

Peasants of Mauborjet asserted, along with many others, that these plants were more than one hundred years old, or that they were the originals from Mauritius, or that they were Pompon de Paris. However, the American Rose Society (ARS) says Pompon de Paris is a deeper pink but was sold at the Paris flower market. Notwithstanding, Rosa Rouletti caught on. A Dutch hybridizer developed an interest in these miniatures and sold the idea and his miniatures to Robert Pyle, a successful American rose grower and distributor. The first miniature patented in America was Dutchman de Vink's Peon, called Tom Thumb in the United States, offered in the 1937 catalogue of Conard-Pyle nursery at one dollar, and in 1938 at seventy-five cents, including postage and handling.

Other roses followed, and other hybridizers were in on the early development of the burgeoning business. Pedro Dot in Spain; Tantau and Kordes in Germany; Meilland of France, creator of the great hybrid tea Peace and a prominent figure in miniature roses around the world. Long the leading source and developer of miniature roses in the United States, Ralph Moore, of Visalia, California, started with mini Carolyn Dean, then later made his first offering, Cutie.

Because success in America set the pace, other hybridizers in Japan, India, Britain, Israel, South Africa, and Canada, along with European giants in the business, have entered the arena.

So much pleasure is to be had from finding new varieties, and money to be made from marketing them, that smaller nurseries and amateur rosarians turned professional are hybridizing. For this happy and colorful explosion, there is an avid and growing clientele.

In 1959 the ARS selection handbook listed no miniature roses, in 1969, thirteen. Today it is impossible to keep up with new registrations from around the world, and listings are limited for lack of room. Rosarians, ever eager to indulge their hobby, are successfully marketing home creations. The American Rose Society has supervised trial gardens around the country, determining which cultivars may merit their Award of Excellence. A professional organization, All America Rose Selections, makes similar determinations of worthy citations.

More difficult than creating the new hybrid, which takes years, is selecting its name. Some hybridizers look to immortalize their children or grandchildren, their friends, or some already famous personage; others try to develop a distinctive "line." Rules for naming new cultivars are specific in their requirements, though not always adhered to. The international code, ratified in 1969, states that names shall preferably consist of one or two words, never more than three. Names must not lead to confusion by referring to another flower or general reference or abbreviation. There are other limits, sensible and helpful.

While amateur and professional hybridizer alike search for attractive new names, miniature roses are sold annually around the world in various sizes from micromini to miniflora; as trees with ten- or eighteen-inch-high trunks; and as climbers with canes that grow to five or eight feet or more. Large go-getting merchandisers and craft outlets offer them as houseplants as well; others, particularly garden shops, supermarkets, and the like, sell only seasonally for outdoor planting, depending on climate and country. Most, in the United States, are sold on their own roots; elsewhere, especially in Europe, they are usually sold budded, like hybrid teas.

Miniatures, contributing to the widespread popularity of the *genus Rosa*, stood proudly by as on November 20, 1986, President Ronald Reagan signed Proclamation 5574, naming the rose National Floral Emblem of the United States.

As you can see, minirose history is not complete; it is being lived.

CHAPTER 2

A Botany Review in
Favor of Roses

SOME OF THE REASONS BEHIND
THE RULES

𝕏

I F   Y O U had been born in time to see the unblemished Sphinx or the gardens at Babylon, or to hear Demosthenes or Cicero, or to shout "No taxation without representation" you would not have seen the Statue of Liberty, the Moon Walk, or the reach for Mars, and you might have wondered why droplets of water cling in such artistic fashion to the edges of rose leaflets after a summer rain.

There are reasons.

Plants in light take water from the ground, carbon dioxide from the air, and form sugar, releasing water and oxygen. This unique behavior, photosynthesis, converting light energy to chemical energy, is the foundation of life on earth. Storage of the sugars makes food for the pork chop or beef Wellington, makes the carrot or potato—or a rose hip.

With respiration, the controlled stepwise breakdown of sugar and other organic molecules back to carbon dioxide and water, energy is packaged in such a form that it can be eaten and used to carry on the activities of all living systems.

Humans and other animals simply cannot manufacture their own food; yet a plant can—and does.

The planet earth was born billions of years ago from dust and gases. Energy from the sun's rays and earth's radioactivity restructured earth's primitive atmosphere into complex organic molecules that became the building blocks of life. As the earth cooled, the primitive oceans that formed and increased in size became richer in organic molecules.

Life, which began in the sea millions of years ago, became possible outside of water when enough oxygen from underwater plants was expelled and released into the air, where it eventually formed the ozone layer which now protects surface plants and animals from the sun's ultraviolet radiation. It is this precious ozone layer, so abused, with which the world is concerned today.

Plants as well as people are a combination of small units, which everyone knows as cells, whose function it is to work for the coordination of the entire organism. Animals have limiting signals, do not produce new parts, but plants, theoretically, can live forever, because without some kind of interruption they continue to grow. And some trees have lived for thousands of years.

Plant cells are typically composed of a protoplast, all the living components, surrounded by a somewhat rigid cell wall. Such substances as waxes, oils, protein bodies, etc., may be found either in the cell wall or any of the various divisions of the protoplast. The protoplast consists of a nucleus and cytoplasm. The nucleus contains genetic information and controls cellular activities. The cytoplasm contains organelles such as chloroplasts, which contain the pigment chlorophyll, and it's chlorophyll that captures the sun's energy.

The mitochondrion is involved in respiration; the vac-

Anatomy

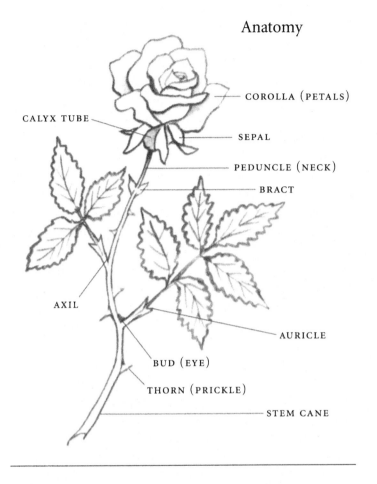

CALYX TUBE

COROLLA (PETALS)

SEPAL

PEDUNCLE (NECK)

BRACT

AXIL

AURICLE

BUD (EYE)

THORN (PRICKLE)

STEM CANE

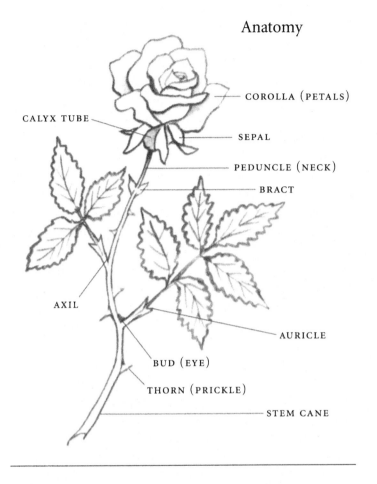

uole, filled with cell sap composed mostly of water, helps to maintain turgor, giving the plant substance. A mature plant cell may have as much as 90 percent of its volume occupied by the vacuole.

Chlorophyll and other pigments give roses and other plants their colors. Pigments absorb some wavelengths of light and reflect others. Chlorophyll absorbs mostly blue and violet and some red, and because it reflects green light, appears green. Chromoplasts contain pigments responsible for yellow, orange, and red; the anthocyanins impart most of the blue, purple and red hues.

Today's range of rose petal colors is wide and delightful,

A Botany Review in Favor of Roses

but the search for a true blue rose goes on, almost romantically. Rosarians will tell you blue pigment, delphinidin, is lacking in roses, but who knows if a plant-loving genetic engineer might insert the gene for a blue pigment, and if a lover on Valentine's Day would welcome a bouquet of blue instead of red roses? Meanwhile, mauves are teasingly borderline, and desirable on their own.

Directed by the genetic information in their nuclei, cells divide and enlarge and differentiate into their various tissues and get to work as leaves, canes, flowers, and roots.

Roots not only anchor the plant into the ground, they reach out and down for water and food substances with many fine root hairs that absorb water and minerals in solution and move them up the stem into the plant. Inside the stem is a system of transport tubes consisting of bundles, the xylem, which carries water to all parts of the plant.

Major elements necessary to roses, and absorbed in solution by the roots, are nitrogen, phosphorous, and potassium, the most common in commercial fertilizers. These plus others in smaller amounts serve specific needs. Manganese, sulphur, and iron, for example, are necessary for chlorophyll function; magnesium is necessary to formation of chlorophyll; potassium especially, calcium, and phosphorous, important to roots. Nitrogen is the growth stimulant; zinc and copper are important to protein production and growth hormones. Molybdenum, boron, and chlorine are also necessary in minute amounts. Scientists now count sixteen inorganic nutrients that are absorbed in solution from the soil by the roots and known to be essential for normal growth and development.

Food conducting tissue, the phloem, carries sugars manufactured by the bush throughout the growing plant parts, including flowers, seeds, and storage structures. In a young plant, the surface area of roots devoted to water and mineral absorption exceeds the photosynthesizing surface; in older plants, this ratio reverses.

If you notice the placement of leaves about the main stem of a rose, you will see that each leaflet is in a position to receive sunlight. Both leaflets and stems are covered with a waxy layer to protect them from water loss, but more than 90 percent of the water absorbed by roots transpires to the air as water vapor through pores in the leaves, more numerous on the underside than topside, called stomata. It's potassium that helps maintain stomate function.

Carbon dioxide necessary for photosynthesis enters the leaf through stomata and is absorbed on a moist cell surface. Uptake of water by the plant maintains cell moisture content. There are even two guard cells adjacent to each stoma to control the action, the intake of carbon dioxide, release of oxygen, and loss of water. The coolness you feel under a tree on a hot, sunny day is due not only to the shade, but also to transpiration of the leaves, evaporating water vapor through some partly open stomata, which is really plant perspiration.

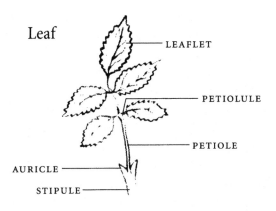

Leaf

LEAFLET

PETIOLULE

PETIOLE

AURICLE

STIPULE

It's one of the major ways water is returned to the world water cycle. Those plants that have adapted to desert and similar conditions, called by the interesting name xerophytes, have specially developed leaves with sunken stomata, more heavily waxed leaves, and surface hairs, to prevent total evaporation.

A Botany Review in Favor of Roses

As water vapor transpires, invisible to the naked eye, it is replaced by water from nearby cells. This sets in motion a chain of events, as one water molecule after another is pulled under tension from the roots, up the stem, and into the leaflets. The ability of the plant to pull water up the xylem is made possible by the extraordinary cohesiveness of water. This transpiration stream is the lifeline that provides water to growing rose tips and preserves large and tall trees in rain forests or in your own back yard.

Early morning after a summer rain, you may see droplets of water framing the upper leaflets of your minirose, shining jewel-like in the sunlight. The droplets are not dew condensation but guttation, excess water expelled under pressure from the roots through special pores at the tips and margins of leaves. Sufficient moisture and inorganic nutrients in the soil and little or no transpiration, as during darkness when there is no photosynthesis, are conducive to guttation. Rose bushes, like all growing plants, produce hormones that are chemical regulators to control functions such as flower production, apical dominance, tropisms, or dormancy preparation.

Dormancy is a period-in-waiting during which all activity is quiescent. As days grow shorter, the functions of the rose slow down. Even though there may not be a frost to retard activity, delivery of nutrients to aerial parts is slower, food is stored in roots and canes, and cells hold less water. The only dependable signal for the rose and other plants is day length, which is universal and regular, whereas weather varies from year to year. In warmer climates the dormant period for roses is relatively short or almost nonexistent, and the plant not entirely nonfunctional.

Ethylene, produced in ripening and senescence, is a hormone to know because of its effect on roses both from within and without. In the closed storage of a refrigerator, the larger amount of ethylene produced by ripening fruit such as melons and apples, will alter color in a rose petal from without, although the rose may have been cut before it

More Anatomy

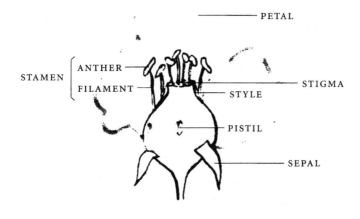

began to produce its own minute amount of ethylene, a function now somewhat suppressed by the cold of the fridge.

Plants do move and respond to external stimuli. A tropism is the bending toward or away from a stimulus as in phototropism, when a rose reaches for light. A response to gravity, geotropism, is the roots of a plant going down, and for want of a better name, negative geotropism, the aerial growth going upward.

Plants have rhythms too, called circadian rhythms, because they follow an approximate twenty-four hour cycle, called a biological clock, which allows them to respond to seasons by measuring day length. The name for response to change in proportion of daylight and darkness is photoperiodism.

Home for the roots is the soil in which they grow. When soil is of proper rose-quality, bushes thrive and feeder roots develop and put out the needed hairs for water uptake. Obvious factors govern overall conditions, such as temperature, climate, sunshine, pH, nutrients. Other factors are location, winds, plantings, and TLC.

About half of soil volume is solid matter, the other half is

A Botany Review in Favor of Roses

occupied, ideally, by half air and half water. The solid matter consists of inorganic minerals, and organic decomposing matter and microorganisms such as bacteria and fungi. Some clay is desirable because some nutrients bind to clay and are held against the leaching action of percolating water. Those nutrients that do not bind are more easily leached out.

Availability of inorganic nutrients is related to soil acidity or alkalinity—the pH. Optimum growth opportunity is afforded the rosebush when the pH is measured at 6.5. Neutral being 7, rose soil should be slightly acid. In alkaline soils iron, copper, zinc, and manganese can precipitate and not be available. In acid soils molybdenum, calcium, and phosphorous can be less available.

Roses can be reproduced from seed, which is sexual reproduction, or cuttings, budding, or tissue culture that is vegetative reproduction. A rose is hermaphroditic, or perfect, containing both male and female structures, stamens, and carpels. Roses can self-pollinate or be cross-pollinated. When a pollen grain comes in contact with the stigma, it germinates and forms a pollen tube, which conveys two sperm to an ovule. One sperm fertilizes the egg that becomes the embryo; the nucleus of the second sperm unites with two nuclei in the ovule, then a fusion develops into a food supply (endosperm) for the embryo. The embryo, food supply, and seed coat constitute a seed. The ovary wall develops into the fruit, enclosing the seeds; the rose hip is the mature ovary and the receptacle.

Roses, and all plants, have properties that permit development from a planted cutting. An entirely new plant will develop, with new roots, canes, and leaves, and become an independent bush precisely like the one from which is was taken. This vegetative propagation is possible because cells contain all the information necessary for forming new plants.

Another method of vegetative propagation is tissue culture, feasible because of scientific knowledge of how hormones regulate growth and development. Shoot tips are grown in a sterile culture medium with the addition of necessary hormones that stimulate buds to form.

Together with the products of photosynthesis, a plant uses minerals to form complex organic materials that it needs to grow and develop. How it does this is not completely known, but development depends on an interaction of internal growth regulators, hormones, and such external factors as light, temperature, day length, and gravity.

To follow the directions for planting and caring of a minirose is to comply with rules required by its very nature that coalesces life and beauty. It's how the world works.

A Botany Review in Favor of Roses

CHAPTER 3

Varieties

SELECTING THE BEST

T HEY'RE on display in a shopping mall, a suburban nursery, a public garden—only everything is on a lesser scale than the hybrid teas: leaves, blooms, spaces between leaves. They're all miniature roses with an irresistible charisma.

Some are so small they're no more than six or eight inches high. They're the microminis. The largest group are bushes of average height, from about ten or twelve inches to sixteen to eighteen inches; others may be more than twenty inches high, though size can depend on climate and care. Mini-floras enter into the thirty-inch range. Those varieties having long canes that reach as far as five or eight feet, or more, are classed as climbers.

Strictly speaking, miniature rose blooms are expected to be 1¾ inches in diameter when fully open, but lines can be blurred, measurements not exact, and rules made before the hybridizing explosion. Further, foliage and spaces between leaves, the internodes, must be in proportion to each other and the bloom. In warmer climates bushes and blooms usually are larger than in colder climates, as growing seasons are longer.

ARS stipulates eighteen color classes, which helps in identification. A breeder has the right to designate the identity and color of his creation.

w-white, near white, white blend	lp-light pink
ly-light yellow	mp-medium pink
my-medium yellow	dp-deep pink
dy-deep yellow	pb-pink blend
yb-yellow blend	mr-medium red
ab-apricot, apricot blend	dr-dark red
ob-orange, orange blend	rb-red blend
op-orange-pink, orange-pink blend	m-mauve, mauve blend
or-orange-red, orange-red blend	r-russet

Considering the proliferation of new miniroses offered each year, it may seem difficult to choose which to buy, but if you know a bit about popular and successful roses, you have a start. Catalogues of various merchants signal E for Excellence winners, roses that have been tested for two years in different climatic conditions around the United States by the American Rose Society, and come up with the highest qualifying scores. Testing involves performance, disease resistance, color quality, hardiness, and beauty. Another source of high approval comes from All-America Rose Selections, a professional association of hybridizers, which in 1988 awarded its first time minirose nominations to two cultivars. A much-used valuable aide in bush selection is the Roses in Review list. ARS annually conducts a survey in which members are asked to contribute judgments of the varieties they grow. Ratings from 1 to 10 grade a variety both as a garden and as an exhibition rose. Results are published in a handbook sent each year to all ARS members.

If you know how the bush will be used and for what purpose, or if you just love roses, then selection is easier. You may like red roses, or white roses, or want to hide an ugly garden spot with a climber, or try miniroses for the first time. If you're not sure, comb catalogues for ideas, keeping in mind that colors in the photographs are not precise.

Consult an experienced rosarian, check the varieties sold at the local nurseries, reread appropriate chapters of this book, and you should land on the right ones.

It is helpful to visit public gardens, or see miniatures growing in situations similar to your own. You can't go far wrong. And if you are experienced you know the pleasures and advantage of visiting private gardens. Local rose societies usually have annual garden walks at which you may be welcome. Ask questions; make comparisons.

A rosarian's favorite minirose is the one just planted, or the one that took top honors at a recent show, or the one that blooms constantly, or the yellow one. It is simply impossible to analyze why. It may be disease resistant, fragrant, bright red, hold its shape, but basically it has rose appeal. Each person has likes and dislikes not always definable, but surely the wide range of colors and color combinations—yellows edged in red, reds striped in yellow or white, lavender, bright pink—are an important factor.

Among the favorites are the singles, blooms with but five petals that open symmetrically about a center of colored stamens, sometimes in breathtaking delicacy. These are reminiscent of ancient species, or wild roses, often found in lonely spots or even in wooded locations around the country. The microminis have blooms and leaflets of the smallest miniature rose size, as small as a half inch in diameter. These are good for growing under lights, with the added quality of being perfect for two- and three-inch arrangements.

Although there is no natural climbing rose with clinging

tendrils, certain varieties are bred to have longer canes, which, tied to a fence or trellis, make attractive climbers. Occasionally a hybridizer will replicate an old rose in miniature form, a smaller version of the quartered old-fashioned bloom seen around the world. These have their own special appeal.

Some bushes, because they are field grown, will produce large bushy plants and unusually profuse blooming on short stems. Very disease resistant and vigorous, this group weighs in for always-in-bloom hedges and color spots. Some low growing bushes can be used attractively as ground cover. Another form growing in celebrity is the tree rose, a bush budded on to a stem, or trunk, producing quantities of bloom, often on shorter canes than those of inground bushes. Not all nurseries offer tree roses, and those that do expect orders in advance.

It is important to have a quality bush to begin with. Those that come from nurseries listed in appendix II are just about 100 percent sure of being healthy and desirable stock. Write or call for a catalogue. Bushes purchased at local hardware, nursery, or garden shops should be scrutinized carefully for insects, disease, and neglect. Not that the shop is intentionally careless, but roses need more watering and special care than other plants, and the caretakers may not have the time nor fully understand these needs.

Much good stock is to be had locally, but still be sure to check each plant you select. There is advantage and satisfaction in seeing what you buy and having it at hand.

Otherwise, order by catalogue where you have a larger selection, and wait the necessary week or two for delivery. If possible, make decisions months in advance of planting time, and order for a specific shipping date. Miniature roses are shipped year round by some hybridizers; others ship only during specified months.

Miniature Directions

1. Buy only quality bushes either from local merchants, local rose societies, or order by catalogue.

2. Visit gardens and check on varieties you may want to own.

CHAPTER 4

Inground Planning and Planting

❧

4a: Site Selection, Soil Preparation, and a Healthy Environment

NOT ALL of the big outdoors is hospitable to miniature roses. The ideal spot receives full sun beginning
with early morning, in warmer climates is shaded
during the noon period, and is sunny again during the afternoon. The ideal spot has free air circulation, good
drainage, friable soil of proper consistency, and is free of in-
terfering roots from nearby trees and shrubs. Roses will
grow almost anywhere with minimal or no attention, but if
you want beautiful long lasting blooms, you must observe
certain procedures.

Plants grown in less than ideal situations may require
more frequent spraying, or watering, or weeding, but they're
where you want them. Millions upon millions of miniroses

are growing around the world and they can't all be in ideal situations.

Miniroses are grown in large beds, small beds, sometimes tucked in with other plants or as lone representatives of their family. They grow in London and Florence, Auckland and Tokyo, Lima and Shreveport, and they can grow in your garden in the ground or in a container.

For one or a few miniroses going into the ground, select a location as near to ideal as possible. If there is but a half day of sunshine, morning is preferable. Where you have no choice, try what is available. Five to six hours of sun will give the bush good opportunity to flourish, but bloom production will be less than in full sun.

If it is necessary or desirable to place a miniature bush in the territory of larger robber roots, barriers of plastic or metal, sometimes called lawn edging, available at hardware and garden supply stores, are easily installed. Or, you can pot the rose and plunge it into the ground just below grade. Whole beds of pots in the ground can be camouflaged with mulch. Each spring, or every other spring, at pruning time, remove the plant from its container, and repot with fresh soil mixture. This is one type of pot gardening.

When planting in front of a wall or fence, place the rose far enough away to allow for future growth, keeping in mind the need for air circulation. Intense heat, aggravated by bright sunlight and radiation from the wall or fence, can burn leaves or roots. On the other hand, fences and walls provide protection from the reach of drying high winds. One solution is to wet down the wall behind a stand of roses on especially hot days; another is to drill reasonably sized holes in wood fences (about 1½ inches in diameter) to afford air circulation.

Miniatures used as color accents, singly or in groups, brighten an all green landscape, or contrast with colors and form of other flowers. Roses can be counted on to bloom all during the growing season. Because they do need special care, feeding, and watering, it is better not to interspace them among other flowers but rather to place an accent group or groups to complement your garden. But that is a matter of choice. However, bear in mind that some flowers are more subject to diseases and attraction to insects and could host problems hostile to roses.

Interesting designs can be as varied as your imagination will produce. Beds can be square, oval, half round. They may be set in a bluestone setting, concrete paving, as hedges along walkways or driveways. Beds can be framed in railroad ties and raised above ground simply by filling in the frame with soil. Some raised beds are framed in stone or concrete or brick. Advantages to a raised bed are accessibility, interesting design, and improved drainage, particularly as the soil in the raised bed is mostly specially prepared. Depending on how high the bed is raised and how large or small it is, it is in effect a large pot left outdoors all winter. Rosarians in northern climates have had success with raised beds by planting bushes six inches to a foot in from the edge of the bed, and by inserting insulation board all the way around.

Of special concern is drainage on a slope where water runs off and very little sinks in. The solution is terracing where feasible, but not when two or three bushes are involved. One successful process in this instance is to create a moat around the bush or bushes.

Average size miniatures should be planted about ten to twelve inches apart (on twelve-inch centers). Micro minis can be planted closer. Note that catalogues usually print average growth size. Some mini-floras will require twelve- to fourteen-inch centers, or more. If you want a hedge, plan on planting closer and pruning more often.

Even if you decide on a large bed, plan to have all bushes reachable so you don't have to trample between bushes and compact the soil or tear roots. First, design on paper. Consider all questions, including size of different varieties and how much room each will take when grown. Avoid having larger varieties shade smaller ones. Watch the sun not only during spring but summertime, too. Fall sun is slanted, and a neighbor's house or tree could influence your reception of sunlight. Take on a job that will not be a burden, so plan a manageable plot. You can always add or plan another bed.

Fall is the ideal time to amend the soil for spring planting in cooler climates. During dormancy months the mixture settles and becomes ready to receive plants. In much of Florida the natural sandy soil is entirely replaced with friable soil.

After you have selected a location and design for a bed, dig out about six inches of soil and place on a plastic sheet. Discard all undesirable matter, clay, dead roots, etc. When replacing soil, mix one third peat moss and/or dried manure or finished compost or sludge, one third soil, and one third sharp sand or equivalent light material. If sharp sand is not available, keep two parts soil and add perlite. For a small bed, mix in a quarter cup of superphosphate, a cup of alfalfa meal or pellets, a cup of perlite, a quarter cup of Epsom salt, a tablespoon of chelated iron.

Sphagnum peat moss makes sandy and clay soil more moisture retentive, softening the clay and adding body to the sand. For a good bed, the balance of alkalinity and acidity should be ideally in the ratio of 6.2 to 6.8 to make all the amendments available to the roots. Achieving and maintaining proper pH is an ongoing activity for rosarians. Although newly planted rosebushes should not be fertilized with nitrogen, they do need a good home base. There is no surer way to know what the soil needs than to have a soil test, executed with an eye to rose health, not farm crops. Sulphur, ureaform, potassium, chelated iron, any trace elements should not be added without knowing why, and just as important, how much. There are home pH measuring kits available, widely advertised; although they cannot tell you what elements are lacking or in excess, they do measure pH.

Much of the country's soil is naturally low in pH, at least for roses, and adding dolomite limestone to raise pH is an ongoing activity for many rosarians, but not without testing first. Where pH is high, especially in sections of the Midwest, sulphur is the remedy. An annual soil test for roses is best if you want your beds to produce at their highest level, or if you're bent on competing in shows. Watch for ads in the *American Rose Magazine*, or the many fine garden magazines, for where to send soil for testing. Local county extension services are equipped to do soil testing, and if asked, may analyze soil for roses. Other sources you can call upon are university or college botany departments in your vicinity.

Directions for collecting soil for a test: Take soil samples trowel deep from two or three places, mix, and allow to dry. Submit 3/4 to 1 cup of mixture.

As you gain experience and wider acquaintance among rosarians, you discover an enormous variety of individual practices. When you get this far you'll find that basic principles of soil preparation are the constant, people and their ideas the variables and knowledge for the future.

Miniature Directions

1. Select a planting site away from roots or other plantings, with good drainage and a minimum of five or six hours of sunshine per day.

2. For mass plantings or garden design, prepare soil in advance. Ideally, mix one-third organic material, one-third sharp sand, one-third soil. Add amendments and allow to mature.

Inground Planning and Planting

3. To get accurate information and guidance, have your soil tested for roses.

4. Directions for test: Take soil samples trowel deep from 2 or 3 places, mix, and allow to dry. Submit 3/4 to 1 cup of mixture.

4b: Inground Planting

DON'T BE in a hurry to rush new arrivals into the ground. Actual planting takes but a few minutes after initial preparations. The immediate objective is to unwrap bushes ordered from catalogues, water them, and allow them to drain and breathe.

Most bushes will arrive in two or four inch pots, possibly wrapped in newspaper. The shock of immediate planting could cause leaves to turn white and fall off soon after planting, which can be frightening. Should this happen, do not fret because with proper handling the new miniature rose will do just fine.

On the other hand, this entire phase can be avoided simply by conditioning. Bushes bought locally are, presumably, already conditioned to your climate. Keep the new bushes indoors in a cool spot or at least out of wind and direct sunlight for overnight environment acclimating before proceeding to outdoor acclimating. Next day place the bush(es) outdoors in full sun for a few hours and return it to its protected location. Next day place it (them) outdoors again for a longer time. Two or three days of conditioning should do it.

Bushes should be well watered at least once a day, more

often if soil is not moist. Planting time is best late in the afternoon when the sunshine is slanted. On a drizzly day, of course, any time is fine. Have all equipment and supplies at hand so there will be no interruption of planting to expose roots unnecessarily to drying air.

Even though you wanted to prepare a bed in advance, and you didn't, it's not the end of the world. If the soil area into which the plant is going has been nourishing to grass, flowers, etc., with some amendments the soil will be fine for roses. Assemble a trowel, large spoon, sharp, clean shears. In a bowl or clean margarine container mix two tablespoons Epsom salt, a handful of alfalfa meal or pellets, a half cup of peat moss, a pinch or two of chelated iron.

Dig a hole larger than the soil ball of the rose. Place the dugout soil on a sheet of plastic. Discard any foreign matter. At the bottom of the hole and around the sides scatter a handful of the mixture of amendments. Place the potted rose in the hole to be sure the hole is large and deep enough. Squeeze the sides of the pot with one hand and with the other grasp the leaves and pull gently and steadily as the soil ball emerges intact.

Place the plant in the hole straight up. The bush should be planted deeper than it was in the shipping pot. Do not disturb soil ball. Some rosarians find it beneficial to straighten out roots, but roots will straighten themselves when given the opportunity. Replace dugout soil and press firmly, always making sure the bush is straight up. You might want to mulch the newly planted minirose with peat moss. It may be heartbreaking, but until roots are established, it's better to trim any blooms, and even large buds. (Of course, if you leave a couple of buds, you'll be doing what many rosarians do.) Make a depression with a finger around the bush and water gently so as not to rock the bush. Add more soil if necessary. Water well. If you're expecting to rely on rain, buy an inexpensive rain gauge, and hope for one and a half to two inches a week.

A bush does not need mounding up when it has been

Inground Planning and Planting

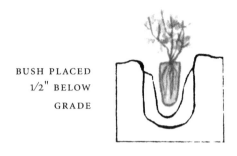

BUSH PLACED
1/2" BELOW
GRADE

conditioned. Any time you plant an unconditioned bush outdoors, it's better to mound it up to about two inches to protect the canes from first exposure to sun and wind. Soil can be removed in stages as new growth appears.

Accompanying each plant is identification, usually a weatherproof plastic strip bearing variety name, nursery, color classification. Place the tag close to the bush, or use one of those attractive plant markers to identify bushes by name, for your benefit, and the enjoyment of your visitors. After a while you'll be able to name all the roses in your garden.

If you are planting a number of bushes in an already pre-pared bed, place bushes at their positions for a last minute check to see how the bed will look. Note path of sunshine, especially if bed is not in full sun, and judge best placement to avoid one plant shading another. Check that all bushes are standing straight, and firmed up, with name tags in place.

New planting, transplanting, and removal of winter covering are done at the same time of year in cool and cold climates. General date is April 15, with allowances for local variances. Tradition calls it forsythia blooming time. By contrast, January is the time in Hawaii, Northern California, Nevada. In Florida, late January and early February is general planting season. In other southern and western areas, the planting month is February, and going northward, planting time is later.

Secrets of the Miniature Rose

Roses are hardy, but new plantings fare better under most felicitous conditions. Rosarians make a habit of listening to weather forecasts on radio or television. If there's danger of a heavy spring frost after bushes are uncovered and pruned, or newly planted, a quick covering with soil, or even a plastic bucket or bag, easily removed, will protect bushes overnight. At this stage bushes are so small, very little time or effort is required.

Transplanting can be done at any time past halfway into the growing season if you're careful to dig up the entire root ball and remove it to an already prepared hole. However, it's safer to do the job on a dull or drizzly day or, if on a sunny day, late in the afternoon. Same as for new plantings. Both can be accomplished during the growing season provided there is enough time before dormancy for roots to become established. If there is a question, you can always bury a plant for the winter.

With a healthy bush that has been in place for a number of years, you may have to cut some roots when transplanting. Prepare an extra deep hole, scatter the amendment mixture, and proceed as with regular planting. With all new planting, including transplanting, pay special attention to watering. To avoid root burn and false stimulation, and to permit roots to become established, apply no nitrogen fertilizer until new growth appears.

Miniature Directions

1. Accustom new plant to environment and site. Keep soil ball moist.

2. Dig a hole larger than root ball of rosebush and place plant straight up.

Inground Planning and Planting

3. Replace dugout soil mixed with peat moss, super-phosphate, alfalfa meal, Epsom salt. Firm soil around bush. Bush should be about one half inch deeper than originally planted. Water in well. Place name tag.

4. Keep bush well watered but do not fertilize until new growth appears.

5. Prepare new hole before transplanting. Dig up entire root ball when moving bush.

CHAPTER 5

Inground Care

❧

5a: Pruning

PRUNING HAS the reputation of being a difficult and usually unpleasant chore. It isn't, however, and it's as interesting as, and in some ways more than, any other function pertaining to care of roses. Pruning is thought of as an annual springtime event, but it's also an ongoing growing season activity. Pruning is grooming; it renews the bush.

The botanic principle governing pruning is apical dominance. When a developed, or undeveloped, axil is eliminated, those down the line are activated in accordance with the size and position of the cane and the condition of the bush. Because a live eye is usually in the axil of a five-leaflet leaf, pruning is directed just above such an axil, at a 30 to 40 degree angle, counting on apical dominance to bring forth growth and a bloom. The reason for cutting at an angle, away from the axil, is to deflect pounding rain and beating sun. It is the job of the bush to produce blooms, which left to develop would use energy to develop hips or "go to seed."

If you do not prune at all, your bushes could grow and produce, but a pruned bush will have better shape, be more attractive, healthier, produce longer lasting and more beautiful blooms—if all other factors of care are attended to. Pruning contributes to the strength of the bush, the substance of canes and leaves, the color of leaves, the color and shape of blooms, by directing nutrients to remaining foliage, by eliminating excess, diseased, and weak growth.

Techniques for pruning miniature roses drive toward specific goals. A major goal is to open up the bush to light and air. Another is to promote growth. A third is to make the bush more attractive. For blue ribbon addicts a prune-as-you-go program is followed meticulously. It is possible, and I've seen it done, to indifferently water and fertilize, to not prune, to not give too much care, to watch the canes cross, and then the morning of a rose show to cut a bloom, put it in a specimen vase, and walk off with a blue ribbon. It may never happen again.

The first pruning given a bush is when it is being planted and blooms and most buds are removed—with great exercise of character. Cutting stems for the dinner table, or for arrangements is pruning too. If you consider it that way, you'll look at the whole bush before you cut, and avoid taking too long a stem, especially on a new bush, so as not to deprive the bush of workers in its factory. As roots become established, new leaves appear, relieving older leaves of full responsibility.

Another pruning process is removing faded blooms. This is not among the rosarian's favorite activities, and consequently has attracted the unpleasant name of deadheading. For years everyone has tried to find it another name: removing spent blooms, cutting faded blooms, but they always end up with the same old word.

Fading blooms need to be removed to (a) avoid sapping

strength while the plant works to produce a hip, (b) avoid an undressed look, and (c) to avoid shattering. Certain of the miniatures will not hold onto bloom petals as they age, but drop them, giving an unkempt look to the garden. Just one or two shattered blooms can do this to an otherwise well-kept bed. Fallen petals can contribute to the spread of disease, which is a compelling reason for deadheading. If you're in a hurry, and break off a faded bloom to prevent shatter, or pull the loose petals, then return soon with shears to cut to a five-leaflet leaf. Always cut at a 30 to 40 degree angle to deflect rain from pounding the cane.

PRUNE
HERE

One reason you have roses in your garden at all is to provide color, so it's tempting to leave blooms on the bush as long as possible. But how to know when to leave the bloom and when to take it? It can be a matter of taste. But an aging bloom loses color and substance as it dries; stamens darken and curl. Many growers like to watch the stages of development.

During the growing season miniatures do not follow a set pattern; growing habits differ with size and type. A three-leaflet leaf grows from an axil; sometimes leaflets bunch up at an axil. Then you have to prune to the five-leaflet leaf below the cane jam. Or, possibly, there is no live eye in an axil and you need to move down the cane to find one. Blind shoots, shoots that do not terminate in a bud, will occasionally occur no matter what you do. These have been attributed to warm days and cool nights, but it does not always

Inground Care

happen that way, either. Simply cut off blind shoots to a live eye.

A live eye is not always visible, even if it is there, either because it is not yet activated or because it is too small. If you see a live eye at a three-leaflet axil, you can stop there. Occasionally blooms do come that way.

Miniatures may form a large number of buds on short stems at the top of an unusually long strong cane, a form called candelabra, under conditions such as plentiful rainfall, bright warm days, a well or over-nourished bush in good soil, especially first growth in spring and last push in fall. After enjoying the blooms, cut down the stem to a live eye on this major cane, and paint the cut. Many skilled rosarians do not paint cuts of any size, but the ease and convenience of colorless nail polish or glue dispenser minimizes the chore.

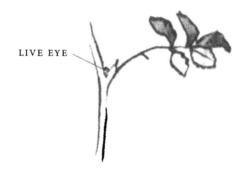

LIVE EYE

Inground bushes that have been uncovered after winter dormancy in cold climates, up to late April, and bushes that are pruned after dormancy in warm climates, January or February, need to be pruned to permit new canes to thrive and to encourage older live canes. Pruning renews the bush, so you cut away dead wood down to a white pith, and again, if the cane is pencil diameter or better, paint the cut, especially in warmer climates. Sealing is to close off entry for disease, to keep out stem borers, and to protect phloem and xylem from hot sun and air.

Secrets of the Miniature Rose

Popular climbers, which put out canes of five or more feet, are treated somewhat differently at spring pruning time. Tips of canes are trimmed to live wood. If you have to trim close to the ground, not to worry because the canes will grow at a good rate, and reach out to their length in good time. If you have pegged down canes, and covered them with soil for the winter, then you may have extra pruning to do at the laterals.

Depending on how you are using the climber, it may be pruned over the growing season just as you would other bushes, except keep in mind that you are cutting flowers and stems from laterals and that you don't want to prune main canes. As the season progresses, you will find more blooms are encouraged because you have trained the main canes horizontally, thus permitting laterals to develop vertically, as they should.

In autumn if frost is not early, bushes make another huge push. They grow up and they grow out. Enjoy the deeper colors of autumn as the sun's rays grow more slanted and not so penetrating. This is the time to cut stems as long as you like, selectively and prudently, even from a new bush.

The tools of pruning are shears that are kept sharp and clean. With sharp shears you won't be pulling skin or bark of a cane. Both small specially made shears for miniatures and regular secateurs are necessary for a satisfactory job. Cute little gardening shears or scissors make pleasant gifts, but scissors type shears, kept clean and sharp, not anvil type, will make the nicest, and therefore safest, cut. Keep handy a rag oiled with common light grade oil, and wipe shears each time they are used. Dirty blades get dull faster and can rust. If by some chance you cut into diseased wood, a remote possibility, dip shears into denatured alcohol before reusing. When using shears, hold them right side up, not upside down.

Inground Care

Miniature Directions

1. Use only sharp, clean shears.

2. At spring pruning, cut out dead, diseased, and crossing canes. Prune down to live wood.

3. For all pruning, including gathering blooms, and for removing spent blooms, cut above an outside eye above a five-leaflet leaf if possible, at a 30 to 40 degree angle.

4. Always consider the shape of the bush. Pruning is grooming.

5b: Watering

ROSARIANS CALL it a big secret, or the big secret of raising healthy, beautiful, long lasting miniature roses. Giving roses plenty of water is in no way a secret, but it is the foundation of success. Every rosarian knows the three rules of rose care: Water, Water, Water. Roses will grow anywhere corn grows, in the worst kind of soil, will make do with what nutrients they can wrest from the soil, may endure cold winters and hot summers, but none can survive without water.

Under ideal conditions, cultivated miniroses live in a moist soil, humid atmosphere, and receive one and a half to two inches of water or more per week. In periods of hot, dry weather more frequent waterings may be necessary. On the other hand, in wet weather, ground should not get soggy. Here's where drainage is most important. Indoors there is always some control, either greenhouse or home attention, but outdoors in the ground, roses are dependent upon random rainfall and artificial watering.

For guidance, serious rosarians place a rain gauge in the garden, which they check regularly after every rain, recording readings and dates. A rain gauge is an inexpensive measure, usually made of plastic, and calibrated up to six inches. You can make one out of glass or plastic tubing that is at least one inch in diameter, or set up a soup can and measure the water that falls into it during a shower. So often a hard rain will give the appearance of several inches, but experience shows, as usual, that appearances can deceive, and there was but a few tenths of an inch. It is then necessary to water artificially, so you fall into a routine of watering twice a week when there is inadequate rainfall.

Light watering, or sprinkling, is as destructive to miniroses as it is to lawn grass. It invites the roots to seek upward for water, and thus, instead of growing down, they reach toward the surface where there's danger of drying out, losing their function as water supply and anchor.

A slow steady watering is ideal to avoid runoff and washing away of soil. If soil conditions are proper, water will drain and leave the soil moist and chemically suitable for rose roots to convoy nutrients. After all, roses can take up elements only in solution. Roses do not have tap roots, technically, yet over the years miniatures can develop one or more roots stronger and more woody than the rest.

Improper or inadequate soil care will contribute to loss of bushes. Disease is another reason for loss. A well-watered bush is less susceptible to disease and hardship of weather than is a sporadically watered, poorly attended bush.

Roses in containers or window boxes need watering more frequently. Time to water roses in containers is a time of particular satisfaction, akin to watching the baby drink all that good-for-you orange juice.

Inground Care

A six-inch pot, window box, or planter, is a special garden bed, self contained and with qualities not inherent in an inground rose. Although the soil may be the same as ground soil, all-side exposure means more exposure, and more evaporation. It is necessary to judge how often to water outdoor container roses. A general rule could be every day, but the variants are many.

Weather can be hot and dry, windy; the container may be small; you may be using a soilless or very porous planting medium. These conditions require more frequent waterings, possibly twice a day on some days. Bushes in five hours of sun will need less watering than those in eight or ten; the container might be plastic or wood or pottery and have more or less evaporation. A larger container should not need watering as often as a small one as there is more soil to hold moisture.

The rule is to keep the soil moist, never soggy. Soggy soil prevents oxygen from reaching the roots. Be alert to your micro climate and you won't have any problem deciding how often to water the container bushes. Just point the nozzle of the watering can or hose at the base of the bush to avoid wetting leaves.

Moisture remaining on leaves is an invitation to blackspot. A watering system for rose beds, whether it's professional or homemade, should be designed to avoid wetting leaves. Where hours are restricted due to water shortages, it's an advantage.

There are any number of watering systems, some quite elaborate. If you have a hedge or edging, you may use a canvas soaker, but these are prey to rabbits and weather; or you might use a more sturdy plastic soaker with fine holes that permits water to slowly ooze into the soil. This latter is easily laid down, and can be made to curve to any shaped bed.

You can use black plastic pipe because it's long lasting, almost permanent, and survives the winter. Have several individual systems, each covering a separate section, as it's easier to get an even flow of water to each bush with smaller sections. Place the plastic T in the middle of one long row, for insertion of the hose adapter, using three-quarter-inch pipe and fittings, with holes drilled at each bush, then water is distributed evenly to both ends. Ends must be corked so you don't lose water.

Elbows and Ts are available to allow you to design your system to suit the shape of your rosebed. For more formal equipment, consult a nursery catalogue, a garden shop, hardware store, garden magazine, or mail order source for sophisticated state of the art watering devices, all calculated to avoid wetting foliage.

Just as ideal rainfall is soft and warm, ideal artificial watering is steady, slow, but cold. Open the faucet as little as possible but enough to get a gentle, steady flow. Let the water run as long as necessary to soak the soil. When watering bushes in containers, pour a little at a time until water is running through drainage holes, then repeat process, simulating a slow, steady rain, until the container drains again.

Some rosarians make small irrigation basins or depressions around each inground minibush, just inside the mulch, but not exposing any feeder roots. The depression is quickly filled and holds enough water when filled two or three times to soak the soil. This method helps keep soil or mulch from being washed away and is especially successful on sloping ground.

It is true that over long periods of no rainfall, dust and spray residue accumulate and can clog the pores of leaflets. It is as refreshing for leaflets to have a shower as it is for you. Providing the bushes with overhead watering is a swish with the hose unless you have only a few bushes and you pour the contents of a watering can over them.

However you do it, during dry hot weather give your miniature rose bushes a bath once or twice a week. You can combine this with anti spider mite hosing with your water wand as you are washing the underside of the leaves any-

Inground Care

how. When the sun is hot and burning, a hot dry leaf is exposed, so avoid leaf washing during the middle of the day when the sun is overhead; try to do it early morning, or in the afternoon when there's enough time for leaves to dry. It's best not to wet leaves on a gray day, and ideally, all leaves should be thoroughly dry before sundown. Sprayed plants are protected, yes, but there's no point in tempting fate.

Miniature Directions

1. Water regularly and deeply. Keep soil moist but not soggy. Avoid wetting leaves.

2. Give miniroses two inches of water per week, depending on weather.

3. Wash off leaves during a dry period and combine overhead watering with shooting spider mites.

4. Make sure leaves will be dry before sundown.

5. For convenience, have an irrigation system if you have many bushes.

5c: Housekeeping

HOUSEKEEPING is something you do every time you go into the garden. Your eye is so trained, so alert to anything out of place, that you pick up the stray piece of paper or twig, the fallen leaf from the maple, or snip off a spent bloom before it shatters. That's if you've taken shears with you. Should you forget them, you can always just pull the drooping petals, gently, and they will come off into your hand. Then when you have more time and your shears, you can cut to a five-leaflet leaf and stimulate the next bud eye into action. Where there are a number of healthy miniroses, there are a number of spent blooms.

Spring and fall are the periods of greatest outside invasion of litter from trees and bushes. Springtime litter is catkins, cottonwood, windblown insects; fall litter is leaves, twigs, and whatever is blown in.

Rose living is definitely easier in the summertime. Still, you're paying attention to watering, spraying, fertilizing, spent blooms—and disbudding, if you're looking for larger individual blooms on a cane.

As often as necessary, clean up the rose beds, not only because they will look more attractive, but so they will not be exposed unnecessarily to disease carriers. Leaflets containing mites or blackspot spores, botrytis or rust, cannot spread their burden if they're collected and put into the trash. As the growing season progresses, watch for naturally yellowing leaflets, usually the lower ones, and remove them before they fall, which improves the looks of your bush, and saves litter.

Attach a plastic shopping bag to your garden supply cart. Collect all the trash while walking around enjoying the view, and picking up a stray weed that pokes through the mulch, or disbudding a cane that promises a good bloom. Nothing should be burned because ash and burning particles carry disease and weed spores, which don't burn away. Burning may reduce the trash to ash, but it cannot transform disease spores into smoke.

After each use, wipe tools clean with an oiled rag, and change rags occasionally. When you've finished spraying, if you rinse out sprayer and spray some hot water through to rinse the tube and parts, you'll avoid clogging the nozzle and keep the sprayer in ready condition.

Cleanup isn't all there is to housekeeping; it involves

Inground Care

dressing up, too. Smoothing over the mulch, adding to it if necessary, removing a cane that spoils the shapeliness of a bush; retying a drooping climber cane so that it will produce more bloom; deciding to repot two cascading minis into a more attractive planter. Maybe you want to "shovel prune" a bush altogether, one that isn't doing as well as you think it could.

A few moments here and there is all that is required, whether you have two or eighty-two bushes. Your reward is healthier and more beautiful bushes and blooms, more attractive surroundings.

Miniature Directions

1. Keep bed scrupulously clean.

2. Remove spent blooms promptly.

3. Pull weeds as they appear.

4. Dispose of trash; do not burn.

5. Keep tools and sprayer clean.

5d: Fertilizing

FERTILIZING is maintaining a level of nutrients in the soil that gratifies the appetite of roses. Roses are heavy feeders and what's sufficient for peonies or impatiens is not going to do it for roses. Roses need nitrogen,

Secrets of the Miniature Rose

phosphorous, and potassium, and the various micro and macro nutrients in lesser amounts.

For best results, and to avoid burning roots, water should be applied at least several hours before and just after servings of fertilizer, including water solubles. Maintaining a pH of 6.5 or slightly higher will give bushes the best opportunity for uptake.

There's too much fertilizer and there's not enough. Too much can cause vegetative growth (imperfectly formed and soft bloom centers), long gross stems, and irregularly shaped leaves; and too little can leave the bush pallid and peaked or skinny and dwarfed. It's always necessary to read all the labels and follow directions regarding amounts when using any product. Packaged fertilizers, available in hardware stores, garden shops, and the like, or through mail order, bear labels naming contents and giving directions for use. There are several good water soluble fertilizers for foliar feeding to choose from.

For first time rosarians, where the drive to win Queen in a rose show is as dormant as a mounded up rose bush in January, apply any ordinary rose food or similar common fertilizer, such as 20-20-20 (percent of nitrogen-phosphorous-potash available, always in that order), just so the numbers are the same for each of the basic nutrients, or higher in phosphorous, but not in nitrogen. Apply every three weeks after plants leaf out till six weeks before expected frost, or in warm areas, before dormancy period. Liquid plant food with trace elements sprayed foliarly half strength every two weeks till just before frost would spruce up bushes measurably. This simple and basic procedure will produce fine blooms, ones that will bring you pleasure and beauty to your garden and bud vase. In addition, you will find that a healthy well-fed bush is more likely to withstand the rigors of attack by disease, insect, and inclement weather.

When applying dry fertilizer, work it into the soil lightly, and water generously, whether inground or in a container. Don't "cultivate" the soil nor dig with tools or your fingers, as you may injure the very feeder roots you are serving. Make a circle about an inch deep at the drip line—just inside the edge of the reach of the leaves—and work in materials. If you have a mulch blanket, simply remove the mulch where necessary and replace. Applying fertilizer on top of mulch and watering it in delays access, and some can be washed away or lay there unused for a long time.

Over-fertilizing can cause excessive vegetative growth without promoting bloom. The reasoning behind the recommendation to feed at half strength twice as often is the theory that a fairly constant supply doesn't give the bush a sudden shot, feast or famine, but keeps it going evenly. The point of spraying a liquid fertilizer in addition to slow release is that liquid is immediately available through the leaves and canes, which is why you may foliar feed until a week or two before frost. Any plastic spray bottle or commercial sprayer is suitable for foliar feeding, but should be used only for spraying roses, so that no foreign matter is introduced into the spray.

There are many fertilizers on the market, some produced specifically for roses. Whichever you choose, watch directions and contents, as some are double strength, some have trace elements, and others contain systemic insecticides. The responsible manufacturer does his research and wants his product to be helpful to the patron, and the law requires specific information of him, so you can respect his directions.

Release of nutrient value of slow release products is governed by supply of moisture and temperature of the soil. In warmer climates soil can be depended on to be the minimum of 40 degrees to as high as 70 degrees, but the mercurial weather conditions in colder areas can foil the benefits of slow release. However, different time length capsules and different formula capsules are available. Should weather and water not conform to requirements of a product, some fertilizer, in an unknown quantity, may remain unreleased and then be released at an uncontrollable time when soil conditions are right—which could be the next growing year. Don't risk an entire bed. Experiment in one small area.

Gardeners with less time and devotion prefer a systemic fertilizer combined with an insecticide. Several of these products are available, and they can be convenient because one application handles insect and fungus protection but may not totally eliminate need for spraying.

As the season advances, plants use up available nutrients, and soil conditions change. With periods of rain, or heavy rains, judgment is required on your part as to how much fertilizer has been leached out, and how much replacement is needed, if any. It also depends on how recently any fertilizer was added, including slow release. If you're serious in considering competition, consider a soil test. Someone experienced in soil testing rose beds weighs the time of year, the kind of flowers, the peculiarities of the soil, and then makes recommendations accordingly.

To collect soil for a test, using a trowel, dig six to eight inches down for a length of soil; avoid including any mulch or recently applied fertilizer. Do this two or three times in different locations, mix soil and allow to dry. Pack off a cupful of the mixture to county, university extension, or rose soil analyst, with cover letter. It's so easy to talk with one person, see his or her roses, and think theirs is the method to try, and then to visit another garden, get a different opinion, and want to follow that advice. What works for you is really the best in all instances, and if you try something new, be sure you understand just that.

You should never see any of the following in your garden: nitrogen shortage, which is evident when small yellowish pale green leaves appear, and stems are weak, or leaves fall off; iron deficiency, which shows as chlorosis, where leaves are yellow, but veins are green; pale leaf centers with dead areas can mean magnesium deficiency; and brittle, brown, or tannish leaf edges and small flowers usually means potassium deficiency.

Serious rosarians get into long discussions and debates about fertilizing until there are as many methods of fertilizing as there are rosarians—except of course, for the basics. Then there are the university lecturers and botanists who insist that fertilizer is not food, that plants manufacture their own food by photosynthesis, which is scientifically true, but rose jargon rises above such technicalities.

Amendments to the soil and fertilizers are used increasingly by perfectionists looking for that ideal bloom. Additions of dried manure, peat moss, and/or mushroom mulch in early spring, and per bush, a pinch of chelated iron, a half cup of alfalfa meal or pellets, and two tablespoons of Epsom salt in spring and mid-season, are commonly used. Many rosarians have private concoctions which have worked for them, such as crushed egg shells, or cut up banana skins, or deliberately left over fish from dinner, to bury in rose beds.

After the basics, try something else. There's always food for conversation.

Miniature Directions

1. After they leaf out, apply to new or newly uncovered bushes (in spring) commercial rose fertilizer every three weeks until six weeks before expected frost. In warm climates withhold fertilizer in time for forced dormancy.

2. Spray bushes with half strength water soluble fertilizer containing trace elements every two weeks until just before frost.

3. Maintain a pH of 6.5. Have a soil test.

4. Do not risk vegetative growth by using too much fertilizer.

5. Set aside a few bushes and experiment with fertilizers suggested by books, magazine articles, and fellow rosarians.

6. Always read labels and follow manufacturers' directions.

5e: Mulching

MULCH is a cover, a buffer between the outside world and the soil. It can be placed around each bush individually or over an entire bed. It provides color, contrast to green leaves and canes, background for the various flower hues. But functional values may be more important than the aesthetic, and far more energy conserving. In very warm climates it is maintained year round; in more moderate climates after spring pruning and fertilizing; in colder climates, after the soil warms up.

Well applied mulch will prevent weeds from sprouting because their seeds cannot get light and air. It will protect the soil surface from being directly affected by hard rain, hail, and wind, thus contributing to a more even soil temperature, and saving delicate feeder roots from injury. Just as important, mulch protects against daily temperature fluctuations that can be threatening to roots, especially in situations of intense heat and cool nights.

During sharp, high, and drying winds, mulch acts like a

coat for the roots and will protect that part of the canes that it covers. Mulch scattered lightly on the soil just because it is a likely material is inadequate to serve its purpose; mulch should be a minimum of one or more inches deep to be effective. Many rosarians apply two or three inches of their favorite mulch for sure protection, especially in warmer climates. When rains attack the earth, a mulched rose is protected from splattering mud and the possible spread of lurking blackspot spores.

Unless the material used is not biodegradable, mulch is slowly absorbed into the topsoil and adds humus as it breaks down. The decomposing mulch adds to the necessary minerals and trace elements in the soil and improves aeration and the environment for beneficial microorganisms.

Mulch is a person saver as well as a rose saver; not only does it save weeding, but because evaporation is diminished and moisture retained in the soil, fewer waterings are necessary. Maintained and replenished as necessary throughout the season, mulch earns its reputation as the gardener's good friend.

In eastern sections of the United States many people use bagasse, shredded sugar cane, for mulch and find it quite satisfactory. Not practical for a very few roses, unless you can secure some in small quantity, or share supplies with others.

Peanut shells, buckwheat hulls. These provide a nice background for the plants, are of some value in the soil, will sometimes blow around if not kept wetted down, especially when freshly applied. Cocoa shells, popular in the midwest, and applied year after year, break down well in the soil to provide humus. When first applied they afford a delicious chocolatey aroma. They can develop mold if in too much shade or too moist, too long.

Sawdust and wood chips have the virtue of being inexpensive, but decompose on the ground, using nitrogen in the process, which needs replacing when you fertilize, so if you use one of these, check your pH more often. Shredded or pulverized bark has made a number of friends here and abroad. This material succeeds in all the right instances and permits rain to penetrate nicely. Often it is mixed with other materials, such as peat moss. It's also a nitrogen eater, so it needs watching.

An easily accessible mulch of no expense is grass clippings. In quantity, grass clippings can be quite hot as they decompose, use nitrogen, and can blow away in a wind, leaving the rose without enough mulch, and the garden in an unsightly state. You need to watch for weeds present in the grass, and more important, residue from herbicide. Dried thoroughly and free of active herbicide, however, grass clippings are used successfully, and often in combination with peat moss to cut down on blowing. The major negatives are the possible presence of weeds and, more important, of weed killer.

Colored stones are attractive for indoor roses, and small or large are probably just as attractive for the outdoor rose, but they will retain heat and so transmit it to miniature feeder roots, and possibly limit air circulation, directly contrary to objectives.

Homemade compost may be desirable, but it, too, uses nitrogen as it decomposes and may contain weed seeds, weed spray residue, or disease spores, and possibly attract undesirable animals in the night. Even thoroughly decayed compost will do better under ground than over it. Ever popular mushroom mulch serves as humus and fertilizer, worked into the soil equally as often as it is applied as mulch.

Black plastic film, also put forward as a mulch, is an inorganic material that does not breathe, creates heat under its surface even though pierced with air holes. It does not offer a dressy look to the garden, and prevents even penetration of rain, and just as important, spray. Film is used successfully in commercial production and in home vegetable gar-

Inground Care

dens where crops are annual, and where it might be desirable to warm the soil.

Sphagnum peat moss seems a natural because it is the very material used in planting and if used as mulch will be absorbed continuously into the soil. It is not too expensive and does the job, can be kept as a permanent neat dressing, is easy to replenish and maintain. Although it can form a crust when dry, a quick touch of the hand or heel of the rake will keep the particles loose, even, and attractive. With each rain or watering, more particles are absorbed into the soil to condition it, keep it friable, and help retain moisture.

Materials other than those mentioned may be used, may be introduced, and may be tried for the features they offer. An experiment, limited to one section of the garden, can be interesting and instructive, lead to an improvement in method. Just keep in mind why you're mulching in the first place. If you have but one rose inground, extend the mulch beyond its drip line. For a small bush, this might be six or eight inches from the center cane, more for a larger bush. A newly planted minirose, and a newly uncovered one, are treated equally. A bush planted later in the season when the ground has already warmed, should be mulched at planting time.

There is one other condition, and that is no mulch at all. There are those rosarians who do not mulch at all. There are those rosarians who do not mulch their roses because they feel it is not necessary. Some do not like to remove and replace mulch when adding fertilizer or soil amendments; some feel they have saved the price of whatever mulch might have been used. They do, however, pay strict attention to weeding, watering, and sanitation.

Miniature Directions

1. After spring pruning and fertilizing, and in colder climates after soil has warmed, apply a mulch to rose(s).

2. Smooth over mulch occasionally and replenish when necessary during the season.

3. Watch nutrient content of soil if using a nitrogen-hungry mulch.

Inground Care

CHAPTER 6

Pot Gardening Outdoors

CONTAINER ROSING

❧

POT GARDENING is attractive by itself or in combination with inground gardening. If you're living six or twenty-six stories up, there is no reason you cannot have an entire garden of miniature roses in pots, or alongside other plants on a balcony, in an entranceway, or window box. Hanging baskets, filled with cascading canes in colorful bloom, are especially popular.

Planning is always part of the pleasure. Explore garden magazines and books. Sketch out different designs before making any purchase. A starter plan can always be expanded when you find varieties to add to your collection. Try one for a while, then another. You will have to decide whether to put two or more bushes in a larger pot, or one bush in a five- or six-inch pot. One bush in a too large container not only looks sad, but also can grow large and coarse.

Do not place plants too close to a stone or brick wall, or

1 Rubies 'n' Pearls
GEORGE MANDER

2 White Chocolate
TINY PETALS

3 Red Cascade Bank
P. A. HARING

4 Isle of Roses
P. A. HARING

1 Hilde
NOR'EAST MINI ROSES

2 Glowing Amber
GEORGE MANDER

3 Marilyn Wellan
MITCHIE MOE

4 Pierrine
MICHAEL WILLIAMS

1

2

3

4

1

2

3

4

1 Carolina Lady
MICHAEL WILLIAMS

2 Anne Hering
MITCHIE MOE

❧

3 Lemon Drop
WEEKS ROSES

4 My Sunshine
TINY PETALS

❧

1

2

3

4

1 Angel Darling
RANDY LADY

2 Nostalgia
NOR'EAST MINI ROSES

3 Special Angel
P. A. HARING

4 Cachet
ROSEMANIA

1

2

3

1 Arcanum
ROSEMANIA

2 Irresistible
WISCONSIN ROSES

3 Sweet Caroline
P. A. HARING

1

2

3

4

1 Sweet Revenge
TINY PETALS

2 Behold
NOR'EAST MINI ROSES

3 Cheer Up
TINY PETALS

4 Patriot's Dream
MICHAEL WILLIAMS

✤

1

2

3

4

1 Doris Morgan
DENNIS BRIDGES

2 Odessa
MICHAEL WILLIAMS

3 Michel Cholet
P. A. HARING

4 Paddywack
P. A. HARING

1 Climber
BARRY BOYD

2 Incognito
DENNIS BRIDGES

3 Lady E'owyn
ROSEMANIA

4 Miss Flippins
P. A. HARING

❧

1

2

3

4

1

2

3

4

1 Little Artist
GENE SANDBERG

2 Baby Cheryl
BARRY BOYD

3 Monday's Child
BARRY BOYD

4 Jilly Jewel
DR. JAMES HERING

1

2

3

4

1 Overnight Scentsation
NOR'EAST MINI ROSES

2 Kristin
RANDY LADY

3 Dolores Marie
ROSEMANIA

4 Linville
P. A. HARING

1

2

3

4

1 Palmetto Sunrise
MICHAEL WILLIAMS

2 Best Friends
DENNIS BRIDGES

3 Peach Delight
NOR'EAST MINI ROSES

4 Old Country Charm
MICHAEL WILLIAMS

1

2

3

1 Mobile Jubilee
RANDY LADY

2 Miss Pearl
P. A. HARING

3 Sweet Melody
MICHAEL WILLIAMS

4 Breath of Spring
DENNIS BRIDGES

❧

4

1 Arizona Sunset
P. A. HARING

2 Moonlight and Roses
DENNIS BRIDGES

3 Autumn Splendor
MICHAEL WILLIAMS

4 Stars 'n' Stripes
P. A. HARING

1

2

3

4

1 Space Odyssey tree
WEEKS ROSES

2 Pink Mandy tree
SEQUOIA NURSERY

3 Holy Toledo tree
E. ABLER

4 Gourmet Popcorn tree
WEEKS ROSES

Baby Blanket tree
JACKSON & PERKINS

1

2

3

1 Dancing Flame
ROSEMANIA

2 Checkmate
ROSEMANIA

3 Sis
P. A. HARING

4 Spice Drop
E. ABLER

❧

4

in a corner, where they may suffer from reflected intense heat and lack of air circulation. Containers on a patio or terrace may be placed on a base or in a saucer to avoid direct contact with hot cement. Plastic pots are not as porous as clay pots, and therefore merit consideration for exposure in full sun. They will help reduce evaporation rate. Wood pots are also excellent. Metal, a good heat conductor, can warm up soil and thus roots. Better not to use a metal container, but if you must, find one with a liner, or fashion a liner from a plastic pot.

There are so many attractive and diverse containers on the market it is adventurous to make a selection; only be sure there are adequate drainage holes. If you find a handmade pot without holes, determine whether holes can be drilled. If it is safe, drill three, about dime size, for a five-inch pot. Where there is already one single center hole, consider drilling another one or two a couple of inches away to avert danger of standing water.

The reason it is often recommended that you put shards or rocks at the bottom of a container is to prevent soil coming through or clogging drainage holes, but these same shards can send roots back up into the container, and then you have tangled roots. It's just fine to pot up the minirose without putting stones or shards at the bottom of the pot. The only time roots seem to penetrate the drainage holes is when pots are placed directly on the ground. It usually doesn't happen when pots are placed on a terrace, though should roots work their way through, they can be trimmed.

A great feature of potted roses is their moveability. Kept in their sunny location until they bloom, they are poised to be placed in a prominent spot, which may be shady, when guests are coming. Keep your miniatures outdoors in pots that fit into beautiful cachepots. When you entertain, those bushes in bloom can be brought into the house as table and room beautifiers. Saves both time and money.

There's no reason you can't use blooming bushes for

your own solitary pleasure. One woman who lives alone brings a different pot inside each evening at dinnertime, to keep her company, she says. Then, she returns the bush to its proper place before retiring.

During the growing season, basic care is the same for potted as for inground bushes. Because more watering is required, more frequent fertilizing is necessary, too, as it stands to reason some of the fertilizer is leached out. Hanging baskets, because all sides of the container are exposed, need more attention than other potted plants. They're affected by wind especially but also temperature and intensity of sunlight. Early morning watering is preferable to ward off midday moisture stress.

In all cases soil in pots has a tendency to dry out faster than inground soil, even with a generous mulch, and more so without. Use a watering can with a spout instead of a pitcher. Controlled gentle flow will permit water to penetrate all the soil instead of running through quickly.

Spray at least once a week, using the convenience can for a few bushes, or mix your own spray, always following directions for amounts. In very cold and persistently rainy weather, potted roses will need extra spraying, just as do other garden roses, possibly on a five-day spread if bad weather persists.

Spider mites are, as usual, the nemesis, and more so in hot dry weather. Plants need a good hosing if pots are too heavy to move to a sink. Moreover, there is always the fallback method of, in severe cases, miticide applications or gently hand rubbing undersides of leaflets with finger pads to disrupt the mite cycle. One superior advantage to container rosing is that diseases and insects have a difficult time traveling from pot to pot, a distinct plus.

Roses in pots need their dormant period, too. Pots may be sunk into the ground to grade level and roses winter protected as if they were planted directly inground, then dug up at spring pruning time, pot and all. Potted tree roses may be removed from their containers and buried. Tie the bush loosely about the middle of the trunk with non-abrasive and winter-hardy material, such as plastic clothesline. The end of the tie should be long enough to reach above ground to locate the place and position of the bush when digging-up time comes. Dig a trench five or so inches deep and long enough to house the whole bush lying on its side. Cover the bush with dugout soil. Add more soil if necessary.

A commonly practiced method is to store potted roses out of direct sunlight, in a reasonably dark situation in an unheated garage against an inside wall. Over winter a garage can house its share of potted roses. If possible, place pots on a bench or shelf to avoid the cold cement floor. Bushes should survive the garage treatment with occasional light watering to keep soil from drying out.

A stored bush exposed to some light will start to leaf out in spring before it is time to place the pot outdoors again. When this happens, do not prune back until the bush is taken outdoors, and then prune a little at a time to not shock the plant. In a short time it will look beautiful again as it starts to bear new leaves in contrast to the pale ones with long internodes.

Potted roses extend your growing season. They can go outdoors during the daytime early in spring and late into fall and be brought in again on frosty nights. In warmer climates dormancy may be induced either by removing bushes to a dark area and watering only occasionally and withholding fertilizer, or by removing leaves and withholding regular watering and fertilizing.

Planting time in spring is replanting time for buried roses. Roses stored in pots indoors may need repotting. Tops need pruning back, and roots, after a few years, will need appropriate pruning if they are outgrowing their pot. This is not severe pruning, as for bonsai. Only too long and tangled roots are cut.

Some rosarians who keep roses in containers on a balcony, terrace, or patio and don't store bushes or bury them during dormant period, discard bushes and start over every season. Part of their pleasure is choosing from the many new miniature varieties offered each year, and reordering former favorites. They also welcome the opportunity to reorganize and redesign their garden.

Miniature Directions

1. Select containers, site, and roses. Plant in container same as inground.

2. Give rose(s) regular inground care, with special attention to more frequent watering and fertilizing.

3. Store roses in their pots in protected place over winter, or remove from pot and bury in ground. When replanting in spring prune back in stages, not all at once.

CHAPTER 7

Taking Action against Disease and Insects

❧

S TANDING AT the ready are the spoilers, the enemy, performing their programmed functions in the workings of the world, without the mind to discriminate.

It matters where and how you locate plants. Bushes with good air circulation, plenty of sunshine, and proper care, are going to have better health and be more resistant to disease, able to survive insect invasion. Should you want to place a bush in a specific non-ideal spot because its color would look good there, put it in that spot. Only be prepared to give it extra attention.

Unwelcome intrusions such as blackspot, the spore-carried disease thriving in moisture; rust, raised dark orange spots on the underside of leaflets, seen, in the main, in the western United States; mildew, which curls leaves in an unlovely fashion and covers them with white film; botrytis, which adds a pink tinge especially to white miniroses—these are the major disease enemy.

Roses can provide a healthy diet for mites and aphids among others because these insects suck at the juices of your leaves. The midge can get into your petals next to some Japanese beetles. Some insects, such as thrips, will crawl inside the bloom when the Japanese beetles are there. Borers will find their way into your stems. And some nematodes can enjoy your roots.

A good defense is the best offense. Spraying can eliminate spread of attack, thus giving you clean, healthy foliage and blooms. Just don't allow the enemy a head start. Present-day research has produced fungicides and insecticides that are materially more successful and less toxic than anything dreamed of only a few years ago. By spraying regularly before troubles show up, you can, generally, avoid them. Spraying is a preventive, not a cure. There is no cure.

There is always the opportunity, especially late in season when sunlight is less strong, for blackspot and mildew to select your bushes. Merely remove any infected leaves to avoid further spreading of infection. Remember to discard as trash, and not to burn, infected plant materials. If you've been away or neglectful and disease gets seriously ahead of you, it's usually better to dig up (shovel prune) the offending bush than risk infecting nearby healthy bushes. This is not to encourage destroying a perfectly good bush with but a touch of blackspot or mildew.

You can avoid incipient infection such as canker (seen as a dark spot on a cane), by surely using sharp, clean tools, dipping shears in alcohol after trimming an infected cane, pruning crossed and rubbing branches, and painting cuts of large size canes. If after spraying early in the year with an insecticide you perceive no insects, then you can withhold further spray. Some rosarians advocate withholding spraying entirely until trouble shows up, but this can be too late and you may find yourself fighting a losing battle. Fungicide spraying on a regular basis is a wise course.

Keep a record of spray date and materials used. It's very easy to forget what you did when, and so simple to refer to a sheet posted in the kitchen, garage, tool shed, or notebook.

Dusting roses is just about a thing of the past for experienced rosarians. The components used in liquid spraying are water soluble, are absorbed into the bush in a short time, and will fortify it against disease and attack for a number of days. Dust protects the bush for the length of time it remains on the leaves, is difficult to apply evenly, is washed off by rain, is not systemic, does not hold well onto canes, clogs leaf pores, and blows where it is not wanted. Further, it is tricky to reach the underside of leaves with dust.

Balanced mixtures, ready to use and marketed in a convenient spray can, are ideal for a small collection of miniroses. Commercial sprays ready mixed especially for roses, are most practical and less expensive in the long run, because there is but a one-time purchase. The can contains a properly balanced proportion of ingredients, and the spray head can be easily directed to the underside of leaves. Available where garden supplies are sold. Follow the specific directions.

A one quart capacity plastic hand sprayer for home mixing will take care of as many as twenty bushes. For more roses, there are larger lightweight and efficient sprayers, mechanical and even electric rechargeable, starting with half-gallon capacity. At the beginning of a season, the smaller container may suffice, but by the time the bushes take off, you may need a larger sprayer.

BLACK SPOT

Taking Action against Disease and Insects

You're dealing with toxic materials here, so prepare yourself as well as the roses for spraying. You prepare the rose by watering it well a day or half a day in advance, and you prepare yourself by wearing cover-up, washable clothing, eyeglasses, and rubber gloves.

Most of the formulas used for roses can be mixed in the same spray water and are compatible, except for Plantvax, an anti-rust specialty, which should be used separately. The stalwart gladiator is triple threat triforine in a bulk liquid, which goes after rust as well as blackspot and mildew. Should blackspot appear persistently, such as during a rainy season, you may need to spray more often than every seven or ten days.

If you mix your own spray, select a fungicide, and if necessary, an insecticide. Put one cup of lukewarm water into the sprayer. This provides a good mixing base. Following directions, measure amounts carefully. Powders go into spray water first. For mixing powders, use a disposable clean container such as a paper cup. Dissolve powder in small amounts of lukewarm water, then pour into sprayer. Add liquids such as triforine or daconil, which can go directly into the spray water. Fill sprayer to proper level with lukewarm water—it's the nearest to rain. Many rosarians add a drop or two of white vinegar to get better spreading of the spray, others use a spreader-sticker such as dishwashing detergent or a commercial spreader-sticker. First try not using anything, as you may find further water wetting unnecessary.

Miniroses, close to the ground, provide a juicy dinner for tenacious spider mites in their life cycle, but they can be beaten. When your leaves look dry and brittle, or you detect a salt and pepper look, and feel something like rough dust on the underside of leaflets, then you know mites have taken up residence. Some rosarians peer through magnifying glasses to watch the jerky movements of the mites.

If you have a number of bushes, before running for the

spray can, invest in a water wand, a tool that sharpens the force of water flow; though if you turn your hose nozzle to sharp, and send a strong water spray horizontally at the leaves, you get almost the same effect. Only take care not to shoot into the soil or wash away the mulch. Mites come from the ground to lower leaves, and work their way upwards. Breaking their life cycle by drowning them is the general idea. Removing lower leaves from a bush gives the mites a hard time, and improves air circulation, a dual benefit, yet it does not always stop the mites.

In cases where spider mites are a constant problem, rosarians use the water wand on a regular basis. If you do this, be sure leaves are dry before sundown, and watch for blackspot.

Sometimes, especially if you have susceptible flowers nearby, the mites get ahead of the water wand. Then it's time for a miticide, an expensive material. Try to pool your purchase with other rosarians and benefit your budget. Mites can develop immunity to miticides, but if you alternate with the convenience can spray, you fend off that development. As you gain experience with your micro climate, you determine when to use an insecticide. But no one, expert or not, makes no mistakes.

As you spray, agitate the sprayer a bit to keep the contents mixed. Be sure to hit the underside as well as the tops of leaflets. With insecticide, spray directly into the bloom if you notice thrips; otherwise, it is not necessary to risk staining flower petals. Spray the canes and mulch and soil area immediately surrounding canes. Spray only once. Do not go back over an area. Leftover spray gets poured into dead ground or is sprayed out, but should not get into the plumbing system or other foliage. Always rinse sprayer thoroughly and run clear warm water through it for a few moments. Leftover spray cannot be saved for a future time because it loses efficacy after a number of hours.

Best time for spraying is late afternoon when the sun's

rays are less intense, especially in midsummer. Early morning spraying is feasible only if leaflets are not wet with dew and guttation, unable to absorb another drop. Skip windy time spraying; you can't aim accurately. Five o'clock in the afternoon can be a calm time of day in most areas.

There are bound to be interruptions of any regular-basis program. Sensible adjustment will protect your roses. If the weather has been dry for a long time and promises to continue over two weeks, for example, and you have been watering regularly, increase the spray span several days. On the other hand, in consistently rainy weather, decrease time span to six or five days, or spray when you can, when leaves are not so wet the spray would be seriously diluted.

Big city rosarians will find less blackspot and possibly fewer pests than the country rosarian; air pollution seems to lend protection to the roses. In certain parts of Australia they spray every six weeks, but in England since the cleanup laws, they are finding they have to do some preventive spraying too, after all these years. Where homes are closer together, you are dependent on the good, or bad, practices of your neighbors. For organic (or non-spraying) gardeners, the stream-of-water method is suitable, and so is planting tomatoes among the roses to (reputedly) keep away blackspot spores. Organic gardeners will want to plant garlic or chives to repel aphids, which may be hand picked, as may Japanese beetles, and spittle bugs, or corn earworms.

A short discourse on Japanese beetles: Many theories abound concerning defense against Japanese beetles who come every year for about two or so weeks, create havoc in rose beds, lay their eggs, and emerge the following year to repeat the performance. Luring them to their death is fine in theory, but what you're doing is telling a slew of enemies where to visit your roses. Rather, if you go into your garden early in the morning when the green monsters are quiescent, search your blooms carefully, and, should you find one, pounce deliberately, you will capture a beetle before it has time to awaken and fly to the next bloom. That's one dead beetle who won't have offspring in your garden next summer. In a few years you should have no or very few J beetles. This works. No eggs get laid in your soil this year. And your bushes will recover nicely from this year's attack.

The reason so many rosarians separate their rose beds from other flowers is not only for ease of spraying and other care, but because of special soil preparation and isolation from diseases contracted by other flowers. Some rosarians daily hose down mildew affected bushes, or pour insecticidal soapy water over them. With a bit of patience they wipe off aphids from buds and mites from the underside of leaflets with their finger pads, an alternative to spraying or hosing only a few bushes. All of which is non-chemical protection.

A popular home biological control is supplying the garden with insect predators. A nematode for Japanese beetles, ladybugs for aphids, and so on. However, ladybugs fly away to greener pastures after they've depleted your aphid supply. Environmentalists are helping to spur scientists toward research into biological control, and encouraging gardeners to participate.

If rabbits are bothering your roses, try sprinkling baby powder over the mulch. Having a dog around helps keep away nibbling deer. Those who prefer to follow a complete non-chemical gardening program or a modified program will find an aphid or two, a blackspot or so, or possibly more, and mildew or rust here and there. Rosarians as a group are frequently organic gardeners in theory, but spray their roses, looking for perfection.

Taking Action against Disease and Insects

Miniature Directions

1. Set up a preventive spray program before trouble starts. Spray weekly. Keep records.

2. Maintain clean beds.

3. Protect the person as well as the rose.

4. For a few bushes, use pre-mixed convenience can; otherwise mix spray according to directions. Add insecticide if necessary.

5. Non-spraying rosarians wash off mites and mildew, hand pick insects, interplant vegetables and flowers.

CHAPTER 8

Winter Care

A LMOST INSTINCTIVELY rosarians pay attention
to weather and weather forecasts, to frost dates, rainfall, and high winds, only to better care for their
roses. Winter can bring snow, cold, ice, frost, or rainy season, plus intermediate variations. Miniroses can survive it
all—with a little help from the rosarian.

Cold of winter is not the real danger for rose bushes. It
is, rather, daily and periodic temperature variations or the
alternate freezing and thawing which takes place in January
or March; the false spring that deceives the waiting buds on
lilac, forsythia, and wild plums. Danger also lies in extended
dry periods, in unobstructed sunshine and biting winds hit-
ting exposed canes and taking moisture in their wake. It is
virtually impossible to protect a planted bush from cold per
se; so the real objective is protection from other hazards,
winter and post winter.

Since the minirose's mission is to keep on growing, it will
put out new growth at every opportunity. When you prune,

when you feed and water, and when the sun shines, the rose is encouraged. For all climate zones, the process of discouraging late new tender growth is somewhat the same, and the reasons are the same: don't let the bush work on new growth in vain. Shorter fall days signal it to slow down in production and to start storing food for its spring push, but with your help it can do a better job.

A healthy bush has a greater chance of survival than one in some degree of stress. Last feeding for your inground bushes should be several weeks before expected frost or dormant period. Fall applications of a tablespoon of superphosphate per bush and pieces of banana peel throughout the bed will build up nutrient value for the following spring and further into the future. Foliar feeding, absorbed so soon after contact, may be continued. In warmer climates where more nitrogen is needed, the last feeding is just before fall bloom. Daylight is progressively less so that leaves are not manufacturing their food so energetically, but starting in January they begin to make use of the increase in sun and daylight.

Bushes do not become dormant all at once, and a sudden freeze may take you and them by surprise. Farmer's Almanac will not always give you the answers you want, though some people swear by it. If frost comes late, your miniroses will bloom later into fall, although leaflets seem a bit stiff as they harden off, and it might take longer for a bud to open, or it might not open.

There are differing opinions about how to cut blooms in fall so as not to encourage growth. One school recommends pulling off petals and not cutting any blooms, allowing hips to form; another group says it makes no difference, cut any length stem you want, the bush is hardening off anyhow; another group says cut only short stems. If you cut the bloom to a three-leaflet leaf you have it both ways. You don't stimulate growth very much, and there is no unsightly cane.

Blackspot spores and some insects overwinter in the

bush or soil, and scientists now offer evidence that mildew also overwinters. A spray with lime sulphur or dormant oil or anti-desiccant is intended to fend off any invasions. Directions for these are precise and should be followed exactly. Many rosarians rely on dormant spray, applying it just before winter covering or early spring after uncovering and pruning, and before growth starts. However, using increased strength of regular spray incorporating fungicide and insecticide, and omitting foliar fertilizer, applied in fall, and again in spring to soil and still dormant canes, is just as effective and avoids risk of clogging pores.

The simplest method of winter protection is to mound up the new minirose with a few inches of soil and feel secure for the winter dormant period. Gradual unmounding in spring after danger of heavy frost is past will bring a healthy bush into new growth. However, where there is a group of experienced rosarians from different climates and microclimates involving large numbers of miniroses, there is always a variety of methods put forward.

In areas where winter temperatures are cold but do not approach ten degrees Fahrenheit, rosarians use fallen oak leaves (most other leaves mat and rot) or sometimes nothing. In warmer climates you can remove spent blooms, defoliate bushes, limit watering. Rosarians in warmer climates don't bother with this, but prune their plants in late January, sometimes earlier, or early February in preparation for spring bloom.

The most commonly used method in colder regions is soil mounding. Soil is brought in from another part of the garden, not scooped from around the bush so as not to expose feeder roots growing near soil surface. If you have room, keep a weed-free soil pile out of view in summer, but ready for winter use. Dry soil is easier to work with, but if it's damp, fill a pail or two with soil and bring into the garage or shelter to dry. If you must work with wet or soggy soil, do not place it all at once. Go slowly. Do not press down. Too wet, soil can form clumps, and not afford even protection for good air circulation. Once the soil mound is properly placed, rain and air will penetrate successfully.

No longer is it deemed necessary to wait for a hard freeze to cover bushes. Covering is thought of as extra mulch, and with the advent of shorter days, covering can begin in late October, though many rosarians still wait for Veterans Day.

Canes of tall and strong bushes can be tied together before mounding, using strips of nylon stockings, old sheets, flat string, or other soft materials or plastic clothesline, so as not to bruise canes. Tying loosely permits canes and leaves to continue their job of dormantizing (Ralph Moore's word) and eases the job of mounding up. After tying, mound up the bush about two-thirds the height of the canes; or you can apply collars and fill these with soil brought from elsewhere.

Collars conserve work, time, soil, and the bush because they contain the soil so that rain, wind, and snow do not wear down the mound. The mound remains intact until spring, and is easier to apply and remove. There are flexible plastic fences available by mail order or at garden outlets, which encircle the bush, and will hold the soil in place. Should you decide to make your own collars, use only porous material; otherwise you risk losing air circulation. Hardware cloth is durable and reusable year after year, but is hard to handle.

A no-expense and simple way to fashion a collar is to use two sheets of newspaper, folded lengthwise. Staple folded sheets where necessary to achieve desired circumference and height, which might be anywhere from six to ten inches, depending on the size of the bush. The folded edge should be up. The four thicknesses are strong enough to go through a severe winter, and while you wouldn't call these decorative sculptures, they work. In addition, when uncovering time comes, they're disposable and recyclable.

Still another possibility is to mound up with an inch or

Secrets of the Miniature Rose

so of soil and possibly some aged manure, encircle an entire bed with a fence of, for example, hardware cloth, and fill the bed with oak or other hardwood leaves only, because they will not mat or get soggy.

In early January bushes should have had enough short days and cold weather to become fully dormant. On a relatively warm day when your hands are itching to get at the roses, you can prune the tops of climber canes and tops above the mound of other bushes. This rough pruning saves time and trash collecting in spring and helps prevent harsh winter winds from rocking the roots of bushes.

It used to be habitual to cut back canes in late fall instead of waiting for spring pruning. But it has been found that this old time function interferes with orderly dormantizing, a slow process for which the bush is programmed. Day length is a companion to temperature in the life of roses. Extra tall canes can certainly be cut back in fall, also to avoid root rocking, but fine pruning is done in spring, and on a gradual basis.

Losses do occur, and sometimes there aren't any explanations, although experienced rosarians will be looking to avoid repeating mistakes. Experienced or no, if you have a loss, you can always try another method the next year, or two methods, one for one group of bushes and one for another. Factors governing healthy bush survival are variation in severity of winters, condition of rose when it went into dormancy, amount of moisture in soil, and mercurial spring weather. All is not in techniques; some circumstances or combination thereof are beyond anyone's control.

Rosarians from Wisconsin and the Dakotas, to Iowa, Indiana, and elsewhere, bury roses over winter, or have "houses" for winter covering, similar to cold frames, built of plywood or other wood sheets, or styrofoam. Circulation holes are provided. The hinged and slanted tops can be opened easily on warm days. The problem with houses is appearance in winter, and storage in summer. With good design, however, they can be knocked down and stored flat.

Another widely used winter offensive is cones, which are styrofoam forms for sale at hardware stores, garden supply centers, and by mail order. Before application, the bush is prepared by tying the canes and cutting them to fit within the cone; cuts painted with orange shellac, glue, or colorless nail polish, if necessary. An inch or so of soil is applied to base of bush. For circulation, four or five holes the circumference of a dime may be punctured at uneven levels near the top of the cone, and, for best results, the cone weighted down with a brick or heavy stone to prevent being blown away. All same-size cones stack nicely for storage.

Cones for miniature roses do not always come with flat and removable tops. You can slice off the top, but the domed shape top is difficult to weight down. You can also mound up the bush a few inches and use the cone without its top. One man paints his cones with cheery designs to avoid the cemetery look.

When occasional warm periods of winter occur, cones act as an oven, confining the heat from the sun, and although you have cut several holes for circulation, you may be encouraging mildew or its cousin, mold—and possibly too-soon growth. Many people are enthusiastic cone users. During warm periods they remove the tops of their cones the morning of a warm winter day, and replace them in early evening. They enjoy the advantage of removing tops in spring and still having protection from drying winds. For the thrifty, plastic milk bottles are excellent substitute cones. The tops already have an adequate circulation hole, and the bottom is cut off. Presto!

Potted roses may be sunk into soil as though they were planted there, and then covered or mounded up. Rose trees removed from pots, or inground trees dug up, can be easily buried for the winter.

Before burying, tie an identifying string about the middle of the bush, leaving a long tail that will become important when it's time to dig up. Nylon string or plastic clothesline are good because they won't rot over the winter, and won't injure rose canes. Dig a hole about four or five inches deep and lay bush horizontally in dugout. Lay the identifying string at ground level extending far enough out of dugout for finding later on. Cover bush(es) with dugout soil, and some extra soil for safety. Bushes that do not survive may have been planted too deep, or are in a poor drainage location and drown.

Winter covering is not removed until danger of killing frost is past. Too early uncovering exposes canes to wind and cold, sunshine with no shade, alternate freezing and thawing, causing further dieback of canes, heaving, or worse. The uncovering process in spring is as important as covering at all. It's best to uncover gradually, a bit every other day or so, and to listen to weather forecasts. Many bushes are lost to the vagaries of spring weather.

In areas where winter protection is required, the date of uncovering and pruning is approximately April 15 in Zone 5, and varies with locale. If you've uncovered too soon and a frost is predicted, not to worry. Cover your pruned bush with a portion of the soil you've stored, or replace the cone you've removed.

If you live in a warm zone, you will be having buds and taking blooms to the spring shows.

Miniature Directions

1. In fall, do not cut back canes. Top prune only long canes that might be windblown. Continue spray and watering program until a hard freeze.

2. Tie up canes with a soft material and mound bushes to about two-thirds height of bush. Use collars to conserve soil and contain mound.

Winter Care

3. In late December or January, when canes are surely dormant, cut top dead wood.

4. If using cones, cut canes to fit, painting cuts if necessary. Weight cones in place; remove tops during warm periods and replace as required.

5. In spring uncover in stages at proper time for your area. Spray canes and ground.

6. A potted rose may be sunk into ground to rim of pot and treated as planted bush, or bush may be buried the same as trees, and dug up at uncovering time in spring.

7. Potted bushes may be brought into unheated garage or shed and sheltered over winter, to be watered occasionally to keep soil from drying out.

8. In cold climates, bury bushes or build houses.

9. In warmer climates induce dormancy, if desired, by cutting back, defoliating, and withholding fertilizer. Continue spray and maintenance watering program.

CHAPTER 9

The Indoor Rose

❧

9a: Selection, Arrival, Planting

GIVE YOUR miniatures the great indoors twelve months a year, in a sunny window, or under lights, or in combination. Basic rules are shared by all methods. Start with a quality bush. Visit a garden shop in your area; write for a catalogue from some of the nurseries.

Ranging the catalogues is a rosarian luxury activity to be savored. Pictures are realistic; descriptions are enthusiastically descriptive. New rosarians should surrender to impulse buying. If you like the bright red rose, buy it. If you like the new salmon micromini, buy it. In another catalogue there's a pink described that you can't resist. Don't. On the other hand, if you've become enchanted with miniatures and are looking for varieties for a purpose, for arranging, showing, or drying, decide which varieties best suit your requirements.

Selecting for indoor cultivation involves considering not

only the colors and types of flower you prefer, but their growth habits as well. It is awkward to raise a large-growing bush and a small one under the same light fixture.

Reviewing the material on varieties can be helpful in making decisions. If you've selected your miniroses from catalogues or the local shop, or if you've bought some at a rose show because they were so very attractive, with good care they will do well indoors or out. Rose societies and garden clubs hold plant sales of potted miniatures roses. These are normally reliable healthy bushes and usually can be bought with confidence.

What to do with a plant purchased at a local shop, or newly arrived from a nursery? Remove outer wrapping at once. Keep bush from stimulating direct sunlight or hot artificial light. To condition bush to its new atmosphere, expose it to its permanent location for the greater part of a day or two, especially if the bush is going under lights. In a sunny location, the intense heat and light may take a bit of getting used to, unless, of course, the bush was sitting in the sun when you bought it.

No matter if the bush came from a local purchase or by mail, most important is watering as soon as you can. Roots even partially dried cannot perform their function nor put out new feeders. If you need to keep the bush unplanted for any length of time, add enough soil to the little pot to cover the roots.

During off season some mail order nurseries ship dormant plants which will quickly start to grow after planting and watering. Plants purchased at local garden shops or supermarket section usually are already in four-inch containers, but should be replanted in a slightly larger container suitable to the growth of the bush with proper soil amendments.

When you're ready for planting, a journey to your favorite garden shop, hardware store or supermarket will supply the ingredients: sterile potting soil, perlite, peat moss,

Epsom salt (you may have to get to a drug store for this), superphosphate, a spray can of premix insecticide-fungicide compounded especially for roses, and containers for planting. Containers ideally have three or four drainage holes, rather than one large central hole.

It's not practical to use an heirloom container for growing plants because not only does it usually lack drainage holes, the various phases of care may mar or actually cause injury to a beloved treasure. Handmade pottery bought at an art show or garden walk is decorative and usually heavy and can be difficult to handle during regular care. Reserve these for showcase use as a cachepot. Unglazed, handmade pottery would be porous.

Present day manufacturers for the mass market produce good looking planting pots with properly sized and placed drainage holes in a wide enough variety of sizes, shapes, materials, and colors to satisfy the most demanding tastes. Part of the pleasure of indoor gardening is looking for accessories, haunting curiosity shops in country areas, devising ways to decorate a corner, a table, a guest room. A miniature rose plant indoors is not permanently fixed in a garden bed, it is versatile in the hands of its owner, and stands ready to be moved to a showcase position when required.

All containers are not alike. Plastic pots are best for retaining moisture, are light in weight. They are manufactured in various colors, sizes and shapes, and have the distinct advantage of being inexpensive. Regular pottery, usually glazed, is breakable, and can contribute to mold inside by retaining heat.

Wood containers are subject to temperature changes of the surrounding atmosphere, absorb heat, cold, and moisture, but can be good to look at, looking outdoorsy. Metal containers do not breathe enough, but can be quite attractive. However, they can heat the roots, as metal is such a good conductor. Knowing the pros and cons of various materials will help you make decisions.

The Indoor Rose

A five-inch pot is fine for the smaller or average bush, especially for the first year; mini-floras need larger pots from the start—five- or six-inchers. If, despite the practicality of standard planters of whatever design, you are absolutely unable to resist Aunt Sarah's old philodendron planter or the one your grandfather had in his study on Vincennes Avenue, then be sure to have drainage holes drilled.

Overfertilizing and a too large pot can produce a gross plant, sometimes with few, or no, blooms. On the other hand, even microminis with their tiny growing habit can outgrow a small pot in time. A naturally large bush will do so sooner. If your bush outgrows its container, you can repot it, or cut it back by trimming roots and aerial growth, then replanting. New pot or used, make sure it is thoroughly washed and rinsed with bleach water before replanting.

Indoor gardens exist in elaborate planters, some constructed under the supervision of an architect. In a sunny south or west window, or a bay, drainage and plumbing can be installed, a tiled or brick planter built, at least eight, preferably ten or more, inches deep, to hold soil for miniature roses. The size and complexity of such a construction is limited only by the size of the room and pocketbook. Here bushes could be planted directly into prepared soil, cared for, and thrive for years. Space can be provided for potted plants sunk into soil and mulched, to be removed for showcase use whenever desired. Supplementary light can be made available for use on dark days, or to lengthen rosedays beyond sundown.

Architects have created indoor gardens in various locations within a house or apartment. They design pools, fountains, indirect lighting, and other elaborate accompaniments. Miniature roses thrive equally in luxurious surroundings or in homemade situations where there are one or two bushes.

It has been customary to place stones or broken crockery

at the bottom of a container to improve drainage or to use a piece of old nylon hosiery to prevent the soil and roots from squeezing past the holes. This has been found not to be at all necessary. Without stones, after the first watering and soaking, the soil remains intact.

The growing medium can be artificial or real soil, but should be sterile. It is less expensive to use garden soil that you dig up next to the fence, but outdoor soil harbors undesirable insects, dormant diseases, poor analysis, foreign matter. It is simpler to avoid problems than to cure them. If you prefer to use garden soil, sterilize it in a large baking dish in the oven at 225 degrees for about two hours.

Don't be tempted to buy specialty soils designed for specific plants or situations. These usually have quantities of fertilizer or amendments that cannot be measured and are not in proper proportions for roses. You want to know what you feed your bushes. Artificial soils are sometimes used, are lighter, but require more frequent waterings. Plain old potting soil labeled sterile comes in half pound and larger size bags, is inexpensive, and does the job.

Permanent indoor planter soil would remain friable for a longer period of time if perlite is included in the planting mix, a scant tablespoon per cup. Perlite is stable and helps maintain an air-water relationship in the soil.

Ready for planting: To begin, fill the bottom third of the container you select with a mixture of two-thirds sterile soil and one-third peat moss plus a teaspoon of superphosphate. For the average size bush, mix a quarter cup of alfalfa meal or pellets (rabbit food), a teaspoon of superphosphate, a pinch of chelated iron, and a tablespoon of Epsom salt. Keep soil you reserve to fill pot.

Squeeze the sides of the pot the plant came in, releasing the root ball, and gently pull out the plant with its root ball intact. Place the root ball into the planter, scatter the amendment mixture over the root ball, and use reserve soil to cover root ball. Press soil firmly and be sure plant is

The Indoor Rose

straight up. Bush should be a half inch or inch deeper than in its original pot. At this point, water bush gently till all soil is settled, and bush is still straight up. Add more sterile soil as necessary. Water again until some is draining from the planter. This will ensure eliminating air pockets.

The level of soil should be about a half inch below the rim of the container to allow for a mulch at the surface, and a basin to hold water so soil won't wash away during watering. Peat moss is most effective as a mulch as it slowly works its way into the soil and adds humus. Add a loose covering of peat moss to below the top of the pot. Pretty stones may be added for dress-up occasions. Stake the label so you can read it, and learn to relate the plant to its name.

Sometimes the breeder is generous and sends plants in bloom, and although they're tempting, the bloom and most buds should come off so that the plant can use its strength to get settled in its new home and not be worried about flowering performance.

Occasionally leaves turn pale and drop off a newly arrived and planted bush. It is because the shock of shipping, transplanting, and adjustment to new conditions of air and moisture have disturbed the plant. Should it happen to your rose, wait for the new growth that will come to a healthy bush. Leaf drop after planting usually can be avoided if you have given the plant the recommended adjustment period both before and directly after planting.

After-planting conditioning consists of not putting the newly planted minirose immediately into the sunlight or under artificial lights. Place it so that it receives oblique rays of light then ease it into full light and permanent location in a day or two. A newly planted bush will not need any more special fertilizer except what is in the water. Apply slow release recipe mixture every four or five months.

Indoor roses should receive standing water, which is water that has been taken from the tap and allowed to rest for a minimum of four to six hours, preferably overnight. For best results, a scoured milk bottle, or pitcher especially for the purpose, may be kept near the rose planter and used to water the rose. A tablespoon of half strength soluble fertilizer may be mixed into each half gallon of standing water so that the rose is receiving fertilizer on a regular basis. Replanting every year or two with the slow release planting recipe is best.

Miniature Directions

1. Keep new bushes out of full light for a day or two before and after planting. Keep soil ball moist.

2. Planting: use two parts sterile soil to one part peat moss. Add one teaspoon superphosphate, one tablespoon Epsom salt, and one quarter cup alfalfa meal to rootball in planting hole.

3. Place bush upright one half inch deeper than it was in original pot.

4. Fill pot with remaining soil mixture, press firmly, water in well. Mulch.

5. Place name stake (tag).

9b: Indoor Care

CREATE A micro climate for the indoor minirose with little trouble by placing the container on a bed of watered pebbles, and by selecting a location that has good circulation but is not drafty. Where a special planter has been built, you have already carefully considered the surroundings. In the case of one or a few roses, there are alternatives.

Many people situate their plants and light fixtures in the basement. This is fine if their habit is to spend hobby time and activity there. For fuller enjoyment, try a spot in the kitchen, dining room, or living room. Roses should be where everyone can enjoy them and not require a special sightseeing trip to visit them. Remember that modern miniroses came from a sunny window. If in the evening at dinner you wish to use the bush decoratively in a cachepot, it can be a centerpiece on the dining table, placed in a prominent spot on a buffet or cocktail table, or seated in a welcoming basket at the front entrance.

In creating a benign climate for the minirose, four to five or more consecutive hours of bright sunlight will do, but you may want to supplement this with artificial light to induce more bloom, possibly three or four hours. Impact of sunlight varies not only with season but locale. The combination of natural sunlight and cool fluorescent light will have your bushes fairly flaming with color.

The alternative to a sunny window exposure or combination is a completely artificial light system. Miniature rose nurseries usually do not sell light fixtures, but a wide selection—from basic twenty-inch fixtures to elaborate tiers, pyramids, and small greenhouses—is available through flower and seed catalogue houses, garden centers, hardware stores, department stores, all suitable for a number of miniroses. A handy person can construct a fixture of two twenty-inch bulbs and provide a means for adjusting their height. Fixtures may be attached to a ceiling track or pulley or hook, may stand on a table shelf, or counter. All fluorescent lights are not the same. Some plants require warm bulbs, but roses prefer cool bulbs.

Ideally, the fluorescent bulbs should be three to four inches above the tips of the bushes. If lights are too far above the bush, canes will become gangly in striving for light, and will, consequently, tend to be weak and not very productive. Too close, touching the bulb will burn buds and leaflet tips, even with cool bulbs. As plants grow unevenly and cannot be counted on to perform uniformly, put taller-growing plants in one grouping, shorter in another, and make changes as necessary. In the case of a fixture that is not adjustable, the height can be set for the tallest bushes and the shorter ones raised on an inverted cup or other improvised platform.

Obtain a timer if you don't already have one, connect it to your system, and set it for sixteen hours if you are not using sunlight in conjunction with the system. Sixteen hours per day should give you a blooming healthy bush. An advantage of an artificial light system is that you can select its location and not be bound by window and sunlight availability.

It is impossible to maintain an all-the-time proper temperature in any home that is not a greenhouse. A cool atmosphere is best, somewhere around 65 degrees Fahrenheit, but most people keep their homes warmer than this, and as it is your home, the roses will have to adjust. Try for the optimum situation. On occasion you may have a rose that doesn't produce as it should, or you may lose one here and there. This attrition is a familiar and a sometimes really desirable part of the pattern, as a rosarian is forever finding a rose he wishes he had, for which there is no room.

Accessories for the indoor garden are virtually unlimited,

The Indoor Rose

and practical supplies for the queen of flowers are easily obtainable. A large flat plastic "tray" that fits under a twenty-inch bulb fixture will hold your pots comfortably, and render plants portable at watering, bathing, and spraying time. Line the bottom of the tray with small pebbles almost covered with water. In so doing you are keeping your roses in a moist situation. Use of saucers prevents roots from seeking water in the tray of wet pebbles and consequently growing through drainage holes. Add a tablespoon of bleach to pebbles every two weeks to maintain water freshness. Add water as necessary. Use only the smallest pebbles so that you have a larger surface of wetness. Include a few colored stones or figurines for decoration. Use replanting time to wash tray and pebbles in hot soapy water before replacing replanted plants.

Rotate plants in the tray every few days or each time you water, as the ends of the fluorescent bulbs do not have the power of the rest of the bulb surface. Too many plants under a light fixture will soon crowd the leaves or be so prolific that some leaflets will be unable to receive their share of light. With only one twenty-inch light fixture and one tray there should be room for three or possibly four pots, depending on size.

Where space is at a premium, one well-chosen minirose bush on a plastic saucer in a dish of wet pebbles can bring blooming color to a sunny kitchen or living room window. If you think it's unsightly, you can always eliminate the wet pebbles, though you will lose the moist situation. Leaves should not touch the cold glass of a window or overheated glass where sunshine penetrates, though insulated glass of a picture window should be safe.

Outdoor weather conditions will affect your indoor bushes unless your environment is perfectly insulated. During outdoor dry and windy spells, be alert to water evaporation in your tray, and during humid, rainy, and snowy weather, check soil carefully before watering. Soil should be kept moist, but soggy soil prevents oxygen from reaching the roots. You can always omit a watering, indoors as you would outdoors.

City treated water may be beneficial for the humans for whom it is intended, but not salubrious for the rose bush in the window. Fill a pitcher with enough water to take care of your bushes, let it stand at least four hours, or overnight, to allow municipal additives to settle. Meanwhile treated water will soften and become room temperature (see page 78). This favorite method is an attempt to simulate rain water. And there are those rosarians who collect rain water.

For regular watering, place plants in sink. Pour standing water gently over soil without wetting leaves until water is draining from pot. The easiest way to water "gently" is to use a plastic watering "can" with a long narrow curved spout, available at nursery centers. It's possible to wash away the mulch and planting soil, which is why you pour gently. Also, slow pouring prevents rush-through and promotes soaking. All soil should be wet. Allow pots to sit in the sink until they have drained completely, then return them to their saucers. The usually recommended misting for house plants is not for miniature roses.

Every two or three weeks turn this ritual into a rose bath. Bathing contributes to good substance and hence longer lasting blooms and cut flowers. Bathing is an anticipator, discouraging spider mite incursions before they develop. It's also the only feasible indoor substitute for rain and wind and fog and mist and snow and dew.

Using a piece of aluminum foil larger than the soil surface of the pot, make a slit from the side to the center and slide foil over the entire surface of the soil. The slit should permit you to cover soil of pot. With pot upside down, and holding foil securely, let cool not cold water run at moderate force over underside of leaflets. This is something you cannot do for a garden rose. Allow time for leaves to dry before dark or lights turn-off time.

The Indoor Rose

Regular watering can be combined with fertilizing every two weeks. Good for indoor roses is water soluble fertilizer laced with trace elements. Several brands are on the market, some already in solution, and some in powder form. Buy a balanced formula, not too high in nitrogen, and higher in phosphorous. Feed generally every two weeks, at half the recommended strength. Prepare sufficient mixture to water plants well. Allow to drain. For an alternate fertilizing method, see Chapter 9a, using the recipe. Always think less fertilizer, not more, to avoid vegetative growth. Every home situation is different.

Daily care consists of looking over the indoor garden, enjoying the progress of each plant, becoming familiar with growth habits, leaflet shapes, bloom colors. If there are no other plants in the same room, or in the house, it is possible to go for an entire winter without spraying. However, if you're not sure, spray once a month. Remove bushes to a safe place that has plenty of air circulation. Don't risk staining carpeting or breathing in floating spray. Spray the day after, or at least four hours after a watering or bathing, when leaves are turgid, to avoid leaf burn. Be sure to reach undersides as well as surfaces of leaflets. The spray can particularly for roses is convenient and its contents effective.

With this care you should not experience blackspot or mildew, but if you do, check for air circulation and overwatering or neighboring house plants. Spray weekly only if necessary. Stay ahead of spider mites—those magnifying glass sized enemies who like to dine on undersides of leaflets—with a rose bath. Do not bathe plants too frequently unless infestation is serious, and then try two days in a row, and wait a week. A gentle rubbing with your finger pads on leaf undersides will remove some spider mites and their webs.

An aggressive whitefly invasion can be treated by bathing or a special spray, or even flat sticks such as tongue depressors, painted yellow, smeared with Vaseline and placed

Secrets of the Miniature Rose

1

2

3

4

1 Suzy
DENNIS BRIDGES

2 Mini Tango
MICHAEL WILLIAMS

3 Elizabeth Abler
TINY PETALS

4 Kay Denise
TINY PETALS

1

2

3

4

1 Ruby
GENE SANDBERG

2 Providence
ROSEMANIA

3 Hurdy Gurdy
P. A. HARING

4 Giggles
DR. JAMES HERING

1 Golden Beryl
GEORGE MANDER

2 Hot Tamale
DR. JAMES HERING

3 X-Rated
DR. JAMES HERING

4 Luis Desamero
DR. JAMES HERING

1

2

3

4

1 Soroptimist International
DR. JAMES HERING

2 Fairhope
DR. JAMES HERING

3 Ace of Diamonds
DR. JAMES HERING

4 Starina
DR. JAMES HERING

1 Simon Robinson
DR. JAMES HERING

2 Amber Star
GEORGE MANDER

1 Josh
TINY PETALS

2 Child's Play
NOR'EAST MINI ROSES

3 Baby Boomer
DR. JAMES HERING

4 Ferrin
ROSEMANIA

❧

1

2

3

4

1 Scentsational
NOR'EAST MINI ROSES

2 Silverhill
DR. JAMES HERING

3 Amber Sunset
GEORGE MANDER

4 Neon Cowboy
WEEKS ROSES

❧

1 Ralph Moore
NOR'EAST MINI ROSES

2 Conundrum
ROSEMANIA

3 Heidi
BARRY BOYD

4 Olympic Gold
DR. JAMES HERING

❧

1

3

2

4

1 Bee's Knees
STEVE SINGER

2 Charmed
P. A. HARING

3 Fancy Pants
STEVE SINGER

4 Aliena
ROSEMANIA

2

3

1

4

1 Gala
E. ABLER

2 Fortune Cookie
E. ABLER

3 Pride 'n' Joy
AARS

4 Party Girl
E. ABLER

1

2

3

4

1 Ultimate Pleasure
TINY PETALS

2 Amy Grant
ROSEMANIA

3 Little Carol
TINY PETALS

4 New Beginning
AARS

✃

1

2

3

1 Ellamae
E. ABLER

2 Starship
P. A. HARING

3 Fall Festival
P. A. HARING

4 Pucker Up
P. A. HARING

4

1

2

3

4

1 Debut
AARS

2 Ruby Slippers
WEEKS ROSES

3 Ichiro
MITCHIE MOE

4 Mitchie's Gold
RICH BAER

❧

1

2

3

4

1 Bubble Gum
LARRY BUSTER

2 Live Wire
RANDY LADY

3 Gizmo
WEEKS ROSES

4 Grace Seward
RANDY LADY

1 Ina
RANDY LADY

2 Orange Sunset
GEORGE MANDER

3 Cherry Cordial
P. A. HARING

4 Essie Lee
RANDY LADY

1

2

1 Sandy Lundberg
RANDY LADY

2 Climbing Rainbow's End
NOR'EAST MINI ROSES

nearby. However, it may be easier to discard an infested bush rather than risk exposing all bushes. Some house plants seem to attract whitefly, which then share them with neighboring miniature roses.

Keep pots clean. Pick off tainted leaflets. Prune spent blooms, crossed and too-long canes. Take care of your shears and other tools. A small oiled rag kept in a plastic baggy nearby will save a good deal of trouble—if you wipe blades clean each time you use the shears. Use tweezers to pick up fallen leaflets.

Going into their second year, healthy roses will perform even better if given a rest, a period in which they store food and energy and have almost no activity at all. Late fall is best because it is the natural time. Indoor roses, although they respond to outdoor climate, will not enter a dormant period without encouragement.

If they are removed to a cool unlighted place where there is adequate circulation, not a closet, but an enclosed un-heated porch, an unheated garage, or the bottom shelf of a refrigerator that is not maintained under 36 degrees, and most water and all fertilizer are withheld, bushes should become semi-dormant. Only the smallest amount of water is required, enough to keep the soil slightly damp. The bush might put out a set of pale leaves, which can be cut back later on.

Eight or ten weeks is enough rest; time to begin again. Replant using method described in Chapter 9a. Cut back too long roots. Prune weak aerial growth. Return plants to their saucers under lights or sunny window and resume regular daily care. A dormant period is not absolutely necessary. Many rose bushes in sunny California bloom for some years without a real dormant period. Why not in your home.

Miniature Directions

1. Situate plants where they can be enjoyed.

2. Plant bushes in sterile soil.

3. Provide light and air in sunny window five or more consecutive hours per day, or under cool lights for sixteen hours. Provide humidity by placing pots on saucers over wet pebbles.

4. Water and bathe bush regularly. Spray as necessary.

5. Fertilize on a continuing basis.

6. Prune regularly.

Secrets of the Miniature Rose

CHAPTER 10

Living with Miniatures

10a: Show Time

ENTER YOUR roses in a show? Of course. You've been preparing since the moment you chose your miniature bush and put it in the ground. The rest is simply dressing up a good rose. The following suggestions and descriptions apply just as well to grooming your miniroses for a bouquet or arrangement, for photographing, for exhibition at home, church, work place, rose society, or garden club show.

Rules and information are contained in the show schedule; see examples in Chapter 11, which are fairly typical, to give you an idea of what to expect. Individual schedules do vary in number and order of classes, or specific requirements. In most cases schedules are available in advance of show time. Rose show rules are bound to be more stringent vis-à-vis rose quality than other group rules, but boning up on their methods will help lead you to a blue ribbon in any garden club or state fair competition.

Everyone wants to try for miniature queen, but that's not the whole rose society show by any means. A spray is delightful, and if you must have a trophy, there are trophies for sprays, for several varieties matched, a perfect bloom floating in a bowl, or three specimens of one variety in stages of development. There are ribbons and trophies for an English or American box, which is an oblong box several inches high with holes spaced for tubes below the surface to contain stems for six, nine, or twelve matched and lovely blooms. The rules may or may not permit foliage.

Just about every rose society show schedule in the country has classes for miniature arrangements. American Rose Society rules are adhered to and state that the largest of the arrangements may be ten inches overall—in height, width, depth. The smallest is usually three inches overall. Sometimes arrangers borrow roses to have enough to complete a design, but rose societies seem to expect miniatures to be arranger grown. Some societies require ARS or society membership in the arrangement section—an opportunity for the new exhibitor to sign up.

Experience does refine and direct your skills, and if you know what is expected, you can compete with the best, but nothing will help you like visiting shows and entering specimens. Horticulture entries must be exhibitor and outdoor garden grown. The bloom should be at its most perfect phase of beauty, a condition that varies with the variety of minirose. Some are at their best when fully open, stamens fresh and of good color, or hybrid tea-like, when one-half to three-fourths open; some are called decoratives because they lack the high pointed center. Each entry is judged by its own varietal standard, not always spelled out, but experienced empirically.

Form is a major factor in determining the worth of a show bloom. Out of 100 points, it rates 25. Ideal form is defined as a high pointed center from which petals unfurl evenly in symmetry to a circular outline, when the bloom is from one-half to three-quarters open. Only blooms with this form can achieve queen in an ARS show. So-called decorative form has a rather flat top that is neither high nor pointed but neither do the petals form a center ball or division; they unfurl evenly from a well-formed center. Decorative minis are used in bouquets and arrangements and can win blue ribbons in classes for sprays, in competition with others of their variety, and other classes. The third type of form is single, the five- to twelve-petaled rose, whose petals reach outward from the central stamens that should be in good color, thus witnessing their freshness. The several varieties bearing old rose form may be exhibited in the specimen classes also.

Petal color, counting for 20 points of the 100, is expected to be clear and true to the variety, without streaks or blotches. Remaining points are 20 for stem and foliage, 15 for substance, and 10 for size. A healthy, well cared for bush is going to produce strong foliage with plenty of water and food in its cells. Ten points for size come down to us from hybrid tea judging and are used to judge a bloom's appropriateness to its foliage and variety. Petiteness is desirable, but a dwarfed bloom is not the answer; the variety standard is. The ten points for balance and proportion are concerned with how the bloom relates to its foliage. It's like dressing for a party and looking good in your new well-fitting clothes.

Specimens must have enough foliage to frame the bloom attractively. It is not expected that all varieties will have a five-leaflet leaf near the bloom, and many will not. Smaller blooms require less foliage to balance than do the larger ones, but always use your aesthetic sense when cutting. Cut before the bloom has reached its peak of perfection, before it has opened too far. This could be two or three days before the show, or the very morning. Cutting for the dining table or show table is pruning, at a thirty- to forty-five degree angle, away from the axil of a five-leaflet leaf.

Living with Miniatures

The point of cutting before a bloom is show-phase is to catch it in time to hold it for showing. If permitted to stay on the bush it might open too far and become beautiful—but in your garden. A bloom show-stage-open on the bush does not have long staying power. A well cared for bloom cut before it is fully open will stand up as you polish the leaflets with a soft cloth and fuss, after enough experience, with the petals.

How long to cut the stem? A stem should be long enough, when it gets to the show table, to balance the bloom, about five or six times the size of the bloom, and longer when possible. A small amount of stem is used up holding the specimen in place in a vase. A judge looks for only what is above the vase. In national and district shows, miniature stems are long, too long, some say. Nevertheless, they are long. Dilemma here. You might consider not entering the crush for miniqueen if you cannot cut a long enough stem.

Meanwhile, all during the season, watch your buds as they develop. An individual bloom, entered as one-bloom-per-stem, must be disbudded and is disqualified if not. Disbudding is best done as early as possible. For an individual bloom, remove buds below the apical bud carefully. Use your little finger, tweezers, stamp tongs.

Practice makes perfect.

A spray should have at least two blooms and possibly side buds, all of which meet in a pleasing way. One bloom with side buds is not considered a spray. An ideal spray has different stages of bloom, but this is not always possible; some varieties do not even produce stages in a spray. Three or more lovely blooms is very presentable. If one bloom is open, be sure the stamens are fresh. The blooms as a group should have a pleasing outline: oval, round, oblong, possibly domed. To achieve a good showable spray, watch daily as it develops on the bush, remove the lead bud as soon as you identify it. This permits remaining buds to come into bloom at approximately the same time. The lead bud, the first to develop, is the center bud.

If you have watched your bush(es) closely, you know just when a flower is ready to open. Cut several of each variety at slightly different stages of development. Usually a local show schedule will permit you to enter two of each variety in each class, except for challenge and design classes.

Miniatures, like all roses, have a tendency to open fast in muggy weather, so you might want to cut before the bloom is very far open, but a bloom for cutting must be partly open, showing a good bit of color, or it won't open at all once it is cut. Each variety is different from the others, and in the area of cutting, it takes practice. It helps to take notes of dates of cutting. Fewer petaled roses are cut sooner, as they open faster. Sepals do not always come down in miniatures as they do in hybrid teas, so you can't use that signal. Again, let experience be your guide. If you plan on entering a fall show, let every bloom you cut over the summer be a dry run.

The week before a show, water generously every day unless you get some good rain. If it's rainy, hot, and humid, you can construct an umbrella over your most promising buds and blooms. Place a plastic bag or section of corrugated box over a couple of stakes, but not touching the bloom, and you'll keep the rain from staining the petals. If you're really serious, commercial paper or plastic "umbrellas" are available. Avoid spraying the opening buds you intend to show so as not to risk spotting the petals.

The show may be held on Sunday, or Saturday, but if your flower is ready on Wednesday, cut on Wednesday, preferably early in the morning (very early, before the sun gets too warm) or after 5 P.M. Take coolish not cold water in a pail to the bush and cut a stem longer than show length. Under water, in the pail, cut again. If you lift up your specimen, you will see a drop of water at its tip to protect the stem from sucking in air. Place the foliage deep in water up

Living with Miniatures

to the bloom. Let the cutting(s) soak up water for about two hours in a cool dark place. Take specimen to a worktable and polish leaves.

Pull off, very slowly and with even pressure and in a circular motion, any dwarfed or streaked outer petals. To have a good symmetrical outline, you might have to pull a good petal also. However, this step takes courage and consideration; you can't put anything back once it is removed.

Any dust or dirt particles on the petals or sepals may be brushed off with a small soft camel's hair paintbrush.

Inspect every leaflet; make sure each is perfect, free of spray residue or soil. Inspect for insect damage or a tear. Use sharp manicure or sewing scissors to trim a leaflet, and if necessary, cut in appropriate teeth. If there is overlooked growth in the axils, now remove it with your little fingernail, a tweezers, or a tooth pick.

Leave very fine axil growth nearest the bloom for removal at the show at the last minute. Too large growth removed at cutting time might leave a black mark; it should have been removed when it first appeared on the bush. Some exhibitors leave all axil growth for removal the morning of the show, just before entering. In either case this can be done with manicure scissors, a sharp knife, or methods described above.

REMOVE
GROWTH FROM
AXIL

Axil growth removal is different from disbudding. Disbudding and axil growth removal, if done early and skillfully, leave no scars and no blackened tips develop. Disbudding at the last minute is difficult to do, and might lose you a couple of points, but that's preferable to disqualification for not disbudding.

When you've inspected, cleaned, and prepared your specimen, put it in about two or so inches of water containing a preservative, be sure it's identified, and place it in a clean refrigerator that has been freed of as much fruit as possible, but especially apples and melons. So-called "heavy" exhibitors store show entries in a special refrigerator, not a self-defroster, so that an even temperature of 36–38 degrees can be maintained. They may put wax paper or plastic bonnets over their blooms, but this doesn't seem necessary for miniatures.

The cold will tend to hold the bloom in position, although roses continue to be alive, take up water, and even open in the refrigerator, albeit imperceptibly. Store each specimen in its own container to avoid confusion and to avoid damaging foliage and petals. Some rosarians use tiny pill bottles as containers; others use chemists' test tube holders stuck into Styrofoam bases.

In the bustle of preparation activities where everyone is working against time, there's a tendency to temporarily forget rose names just when you need them. The best thing to do is label the specimen as you cut, either with a pressure sensitive label on the container, a strip of paper tied around the cane, or regular plastic labels made specifically for the purpose.

One method of storing for show allows you to cut well in advance of show date, precisely when you think a specimen is ready, so you don't lose a likely competitor: the dry wrap method, which is not successful enough of the time to make it worth the extra effort.

Some preparation is necessary. A bit of florist clay, hot wax, or even a small piece of duct tape—something to slap on the end of the cut specimen to keep it from functioning, a protection for the bloom, and wax paper and plastic wrap for the entire specimen. When a specimen is selected, cut when the leaves and petals are dry, probably early afternoon. Immediately cover the stem end with the clay or duct tape, cover the bloom and stem loosely with wax paper, and the entire package with plastic wrap which seals itself. You might want to use a cut-down paper cup to better protect a beautiful bloom. Store the package vertically in a container, or horizontally on a shelf in the refrigerator. The morning of the show, unwrap, place the specimen in room temperature water up to the bloom, cut off the protected end under water, and watch the specimen come back to active behavior.

Dry wrap storage means, beside some experimentation, cutting when a specimen is ready. But sometimes it might be necessary to cut a dew or rain covered stem, so after sealing the end, roll the bloom and leaves lightly over an absorbent paper towel until no moisture appears on the towel. Or you might need to repeat this a few times. Don't use a tissue, as it can leave lint on petals that would be difficult to remove. A damp bloom will almost certainly turn dark and murky when wrapped.

The morning of the show, rise early, dress comfortably. Take one last look in the garden for possible entries. For a show at a close-in location, take your entries, labels intact, packed carefully in a pail or picnic box. After many shows, you will know how you want to transport your entries. Experienced exhibitors like to carry entries in their cars (SUVs) because they have full control, and may drive hundreds of miles. But they love what they're doing.

Even if you have an advance schedule, arrive early to allow plenty of time to register, find a space to work, location of vases, and entry tags. Read the schedule again. Oftentimes someone is assigned to advise novices. Partake of the bounty.

At the preparation tables you will see old experienced

hands, everyone from twenty minus, to ninety plus, standing there, oblivious to all surrounding enterprise, squinting for "unwanted growth," invisible scars, ideal open stage. What you hear cannot hurt you, and you will learn a good deal. It is remarkable how the most experienced and successful winners of ribbons and trophies will tell you they are still learning. They are always happy to share their knowledge—during the judging, at a society meeting, at a seminar, at a district or national convention, but *not* while they are readying their show entries.

First position your entries in their vases. If a bloom is too stubborn to open enough, circle inside the petals with a cotton tip or rounded end of a small camel's hairbrush. Open your mouth over the bloom—do not blow—the heat may do the job. Again, work on the leaflets with a cloth. The waxy covering of the leaf will take a shine better than show leather. It is illegal and also not good for the leaf to use any material assistance, but the leaf won't need it. To be typical of its variety, the foliage must shine naturally.

Hold the specimens, one at a time, in the water you brought, and cut to proper length, under water. If you like, use your own preservative-seasoned water to replace that already in the entry bottle. Position each bloom straight up, using foil if necessary for securing the cane. Check schedule for permission here. Have tag correctly filled in (out) with the name of your miniature, class number, and your name in its specified two places.

It is important that the specimen you present looks good. When you take a likely candidate and dress it, cut out the axil growth, clean the leaves, stem and petals, polish leaflets with finger pads or soft cloth, position it straight up, it is going to stand with the best because it is worthy.

Check all details one last time, including level of water in vase, the all-important, correct name and absence of any foreign matter such as your identity tag. Present your entries to the placement committee, or if there isn't one, take your entries to their proper places. There are usually signs specifying the classes. Stand back to survey critically before you leave. Now it is up to the judges

Miniature Directions

1. Practice disbudding, cutting, grooming.

2. For actual show, select candidate, cut too long stem when bloom is half open, cut again under water. Label.

3. Clean and groom foliage. Store in cool, dark place or refrigerator.

4. Day of show, follow schedule. Check again: entry tag, axil growth, clean specimen, water in container, openness and shape of bloom(s).

10b: Photography without Tears

ONE OF THE delightful perquisites of minirose gardening is minirose photography. Today's cameras have removed the technical frustrations from picture taking to permit easier recording of the pleasure of a bouquet, a bee dining on a newly opened bud, or a whole garden in bloom.

But photographing roses isn't a matter of technical supplies; it's your emotion, your admiration for the rose which when translated into your photographs will bring distinction. If you have a bush simply covered with white and pale green blooms, and a few dark green tight buds, and possibly some pinkish ones that are just showing color, you can take people along with you to enjoy the view via your photograph.

There is much going on in the world of photography. No more do you need to lug heavy lenses and cameras, or worry if you need 400 or 1000 film. It's all in the pixels. Five million, three million, one or so million. Take a picture, reproduce it on the camera monitor. If it's not exactly as you want it, delete it. Take another. It's a way of life for rosarians who want to immortalize their best specimens.

The computer age is also the digital camera age. Not that there aren't those photographers who use SLR, 35-mm single lens reflex cameras and buy film to be developed, have wide angle and close up lenses. Yet the techniques of posing a bloom, of photographing a garden, a spray, rosarians at work readying their show entries—these remain the same.

Study the photos you like best, your own as well as the work of others, and ask yourself why. Of course, the beauty of the rose itself will be a large factor in your choice, but notice the shading, size of the bloom, background color, the composition. Do you like the entire bush, a spray, a bed of miniatures, an arrangement? Most people like all of them, and therefore shoot all these subjects or any related to miniroses yet concentrate on one at a time to develop skill in one area before going on to another. This is time for a stable tripod. Once you master a tripod, you won't do without it very often.

Backgrounds take on importance because they influence the colors of what you see. Tan, beige, and peach are the least productive as background color; they seem to absorb petal color, distort its value. Notice the tan against pastels—it seems to sap the fullness of hue. Shades of blue, black, green, gray, or white will show your rose to best advantage. Avoid shiny backgrounds that interfere with natural color and reflect light where you don't want it.

Grass is a natural, and gives a range of green and sometimes with new blades even offers a tip of very light green that borders on iridescence, which enhances a very light or very dark minirose. You can achieve a natural-looking photo if you cut a stem long enough to draw water in a bowl but shorter than the grass, locate a level patch of grass, then place your rose gently on top and ready the camera.

Be careful of what is in range of your shot. Remove shears, jacket, and notebook from the composition. With SLR cameras, bracket your exposures. With the digital cameras, look carefully at your monitor and decide if this or that shot is better. Discard any you don't want.

Use natural light as much as possible. Some of the most successful shots are made early morning when the light is bright but there's no direct sunshine. Sun angles are longer in the morning and later in the afternoon. Roses already fully open on the bush are fresh in appearance early in the morning. It's fun to find dew on petals and natural moisture and sometimes guttation on leaves. So often photographers will sprinkle water onto a bloom or bush thinking they have given the bloom an appealing look. But the droplets that form are full and round and look artificial.

Early evening light before sunset can lend mystery and romance. So many times you see photographs taken in a studio using special lighting effects; and that's what you see in the final photograph: special lighting effects. If the rose sits too long under hot lights it will lose substance, although the shot might get brownie points for composition. Photographing in the shade of a bush or tree midday will give you good light without direct sun and will not fade the color of your petals. This is a cousin of early morning photographing.

The most appealing miniature rose is the one that appeals to you. Just as a person smiles when being photographed, so should you have your rose smile. Clean the leaves carefully, groom the bloom as you would for a show entry. Determine the angle that will best show the good form of the high pointed center or, if you have selected a single, the golden stamens. Think happy roses. Sounds a bit much—but good photography reflects your attitudes.

Watching a bud develop into a gorgeous bloom is a distinct pleasure of the garden. To record this, begin with a bush you know is a good producer. Photograph one or two buds, note the name of bush, date, and time of day. If you have several bushes of the same variety, it can be done with as many as you like. Notice that different varieties develop at different rates. Select a period when you will be close to the bush for several days and can get to your camera quickly. Tie a bit of soft yarn loosely around the canes you have selected so you don't forget which ones you have chosen. Check two or three times a day, and shoot when you notice development. Some buds might take a number of days, depending on variety, weather, temperature, and location of bush. Those closer to a fence or wall will gain heat by reflection, and once partly open, may open rapidly or possibly blow before you realize it. Record several stages of development. If you like, you can provide artificial backgrounds set informally on a chair or held by an obliging friend.

Once a rose is in its perfect stage on the bush, you don't have too long a time before it will be past its peak. In someone else's garden, position yourself and camera as necessary and take your picture. Such an experience teaches one of the prime garden rules: never lose an opportunity. Keep your camera with you at all times, and keep it loaded. There are some garden photography contests that have classes for roses on the bush.

This pursuit is also useful for learning variety habits. After some experience, you know to cut a bloom just before it is ready to be photographed, plunge foliage up to the bloom into cool water for an hour or so, then remove from water and wipe leaves gently with a soft cloth. Harden the specimen in the refrigerator for a while to halt any fast opening. Obviously this procedure will not work on a rainy or dark day, unless you try some off-camera backlighting with a lamp.

Don't forget your notebook, a major piece of equipment. Too many times you shoot a minirose here, one there, a whole lineup, and you've made no record of names and dates, but you're sure you'll remember all the details. Nothing is more annoying than knowing at the time of the shooting just which rose that was—and three weeks later not being able to. For your consolation, even experts falter on identification.

Miniatures are in such large numbers, their names possibly similar to the one you may or may not be photographing, you can't afford to lose the nametag. All slides should be identified, and photos as well. If the reverse of the photo is smooth, place a self-adhesive label on it and write your information. If you're photographing only your own one or two miniroses, careful identification is simpler.

An obviously designed or posed group does not appear fussy or unnatural if you make your purpose obvious, such as contrasting a large bloom with a small one. You might want to shoot a group of pink roses, which do not naturally grow on the same bush, but the picture could be attractive if you designed it, and planned it on paper first to not move roses around out of water on a hot day.

Flower arrangers new to rose arranging should photograph their arrangements for self-instruction. Make critical judgments. Because there's so much emotion tied up in arranging, it's well to put on your thickest skin when you begin to photograph your minirose designs. Avoid serious errors such as wasted roses by planning first before you remove the design from the refrigerator. Use the Hollywood stand-in process here, too: put a surrogate arrangement in position before shooting; judge it for focus, background, light, and angle of shooting. Then bring out the star.

Visit rose shows and photograph other people's specimens and arrangements; bring your digital camera with its built-in flash, or use your other camera with 400 film that does not require bright light. Even if the shot is grainy it will bring you pleasure and instruction. An outdoor background is very appealing for an arrangement. Take a small table outdoors, place certain supporting accessories, such as a base, within camera range, and then place the arrangement.

Many times you find a shot so exciting you want to use it forever. With a little extra planning you can produce Christmas or birthday cards as small gifts that are pleasing to look at, will last longer than cookies, and be less fattening.

One reason rosarians as a group are such good photographers is that they love their roses so much they want to look at them again and again, want to compete with fellow rosarians, and get their fill of miniroses, in the garden and in the album. As usual, there's an antidote for that, too: beckoning photography contests around the country, including one sponsored annually by the American Rose Society, can satisfy every taste with that competitive edge.

Miniature Directions

1. Be familiar with your camera(s).

2. Groom rose or roses before photographing.

3. Plan ahead for special compositions.

4. Identify every shot.

5. Take several shots of each subject at different angles to find the most desirable.

10c: Rooting and Hybridizing

F OR SOME, it is not enough to be engaged in raising beautiful miniature roses. Other facets present themselves to broaden the miniature rose growing experience, offering a different kind of creativity. Hybridizing, which means forming new varieties through pollination (sexual reproduction), can be a consuming hobby, rewarding aesthetically, and possibly monetarily. Rooting is an appetite whetter, suitable for exact and relatively simple reproduction. What you see is what you get. Rooting makes a replica of the parent plant.

It is illegal to reproduce patented roses asexually, such as with rooting, but after twenty years patents run out. Varieties such as Baby Katie, Rise 'n Shine, Party Girl, and Magic Carrousel are out of patent, as is the climber Jeanne Lajoie, which interestingly enough was never even patented.

The ideal time for rooting is the afternoon of a dull drizzly day toward the end of the first bloom period. Know where you are going to put your new bush and have ready some rooting powder, peat moss, a small glass jar, a weeder or sturdy stick.

Select a full-blown rose specimen on a strong healthy bush. Cut a long stem with several five-leaflet leaves. Rip off the lower two or three leaves. The reason for ripping and not cutting is to leave a rupture of the skin, or cuticle, on the cane, where roots should develop. Ideally, two or more five-leaflet leaves should remain.

Dip base of cut cane into rooting powder, and shake off excess. Form a slanting hole where you are to "plant" the cane, using a stick or your finger. Sprinkle a pinch of rooting powder into the hole; slant in cane up to remaining leaves. Fill the hole with soil and some peat moss and press with palms and fingers. Mulch with a bit of peat moss. Water well.

Cut the bloom from top of the cane and place a name stake. Screw in a clear jar over the above ground leaves, and wait a few weeks. If you are successful, you have rooted a new plant. To test, pull gently on the cane.

Remove glass jar when leaves appear and fertilize at half strength. It's best to do rooting outdoors as near the peak season as possible so your new plant has a chance to develop enough root system to survive the winter.

Later in the season, bring cuttings indoors for rooting under lights. Place cuttings individually into small pots or even paper cups filled with one third peat moss, one third sterile soil, on third vermiculite. Cover with clear glass or a plastic bag supported by a stick so that bag does not touch cane. When cutting shows signs of growth feed with half strength water soluble fertilizer containing trace elements. Transplant into regular size pots for winter growing after first buds appear.

A block of floral foam may be used to root a cutting, but it is tricky. Use a pencil size instrument to form a hole to receive the cane, or try inserting the cane into the foam, same as you would in soil. Water well and proceed as above.

Not all cuttings will root, so you may want to try several at a time. Some varieties lend themselves better than others, and, as usual, all the other variables enter into your success, such as climate, soil, water, location, vigor of cutting. Many miniature rose nurseries in the United States use both the cuttings method and tissue culture to multiply their stock.

Working with miniature roses is an adventure for most rosarians, many who think producing a new variety is a dream come true. They have named their new miniroses for spouses, children, friends, cities, emotions.

Using simple procedures, anyone can experiment with hybridizing and taste the excitement. Requirements are a certain amount of patience, a number of established vigorous miniature rose bushes, a few tools, and some room in the refrigerator. Through the ARS you can join the Rose Hybridizers Association for a newsletter and contact with fellow amateur hybridizers, with meetings at ARS national conventions.

Hybridizing is pollinating, sexual reproduction. Because roses can self-pollinate if allowed, you decide which roses you are going to work with. You have a wide-open choice here because any miniature is eligible. In hybridizing, the law does not bar use of any rose in patent because you are potentially creating something new. You need to decide which will be male, the pollen parent, and which female, the seed parent. Rosarians slip into jargon and refer to "mothers" and "fathers," as often as not.

Some roses have been used as both seed and pollen parent, but if you use a larger rose, for example, a polyantha, as a seed parent but pollinate with a miniature, you will produce a miniature.

It is necessary to do your crossing as early in the season as possible, preferably with first bloom, to allow for full development of the hip. Seeds must mature to germinate. Hips take up to four months to ripen, depending on location, will color a dark orange to signal ripeness, are not as hard when still green.

To begin, early one morning remove petals from a rose that will open that day. Remove anthers and place in a clean flat box to dry. Set box inside in a safe place. Ready pollen will fall from drying sacs or can be sifted through a tea strainer into a clean dry box or jar. Tag this pollen "male pollen parent," and its variety name; include date. Keep pollen out of sunlight.

Select a female parent. Remove petals, sepals; discard anthers. Protect with a baggie from outside undesired pollination by wind or insect. Some hybridizers use an opaque bag against the baking hot sun. You can provide ventilation holes to prevent sweating if you choose a wax paper or plastic bag. During period when male anthers are drying, the female parent will produce a sticky substance on the stigma, which indicates it is ready to receive pollen. From the accumulation of dry pollen, using either your (clean) finger, pipe cleaner, or small brush, dust pollen on receptive stigma. Cover again with glassine or wax paper bag to protect pollination.

The word from some hybridizers is that they no longer find it necessary to cover pollination, but this may depend on climate and location—and inclination. Some hybridizers find that even with ventilated baggies, especially plastic, hips will rot.

Because not all pollinations are successful, dust stigma again the next day with pollen from the same male parent, hoping to get more seed. Label your female with date(s), name of both parents, female first, number of times pollen was applied. With several crossings, you will have more opportunity for a take. A successful cross will swell and form a hip containing seed. Do not overfertilize or overwater lest hip split or fall off.

Harvested hips are cut, crushed open, or even ground in a blender to obtain seeds. There is much discussion concerning "sinkers" among rose hybridizers; sinkers are seeds that fall to the bottom when placed in a pan or jar of water after harvesting. Those that stay on top, the floaters, are discarded by some as nongerminators. Others plant all the seeds. Either way, seeds should be treated with 50 percent captan solution to prevent mold. Store seeds in sphagnum moss in a ventilated plastic bag in the refrigerator, labels included, at 40 degrees for about six weeks.

An alternative is to keep intact hips in a plastic bag in a cool place at about 50 degrees for about a month or so, and then cut open. Seeds are then treated with the captan solution and placed on a bed of vermiculite and peat moss, covered with sand or peat moss, until they sprout. In northern regions this step is usually under lights.

Living with Miniatures

Unfolded seedlings (sprouts) are then planted in sterile soil in trays or individual cups punched for drainage, or small pots, for actual growing. Many hybridizers put seeds directly from refrigerator into sterile soil in the first place, and have good success this way. In any case, soil must be kept moist.

If placed about six inches under lights for sixteen hours a day, seedlings should sprout in about seven or eight weeks. In spring, after danger of frost is past, they may be eased outdoors, labels intact, for a few hours per day. Gradually increase the time until they are hardened to the outside. Then comes the fun of watching for promising seedlings, seedlings that might become exciting new miniature roses.

Miniature Directions

ROOTING

1. To root, take ripe cutting, rip off bottom five-leaflet leaves, remove opened flower. Leave at least two five-leaflet leaves.

Secrets of the Miniature Rose

2. Dip cutting into rooting powder, slant into prepared hole sprinkled lightly with rooting powder. Fill hole with soil and peat moss, press and water in well.

3. Cover with clear jar. Label.

HYBRIDIZING

1. To hybridize, select at first bloom a male and female parent. Remove petals and dry anthers of male for pollen. Keep pollen out of sun. Remove anthers and petals from female.

2. When female stigma exudes sticky substance, dust with dry pollen. Tag. Wait for dark orange hips.

3. Harvest hips and store seeds treated with captan solution in damp sphagnum peat moss in refrigerator for six or seven weeks.

4. Plant seeds into trays or individual containers of sterile soil or vermiculite and peat. Place under lights or outdoors, depending on climate. Keep moist.

5. In cooler climates, ease outdoors at proper time. Watch for promising seedlings.

10d: Drying Out

JUST WHEN you think you've done it all, a new form of miniature rose living presents itself. Not that drying flowers is new, it's that drying roses is often considered fit only for the professionals, but perish the thought. Once you do it, you're likely to find it a fascinating adjunct to cultivating and arranging.

Needed are a small, soft camel's hair brush, a teaspoon, several containers for drying roses, a storage place, an oven, one pound or more of silica gel, tweezers, snub nosed tongs like those used by stamp collectors—and miniroses. Since silica gel has become available and popular, and less expensive than formerly, other desiccants such as sand or even borax and corn meal are no longer commonly used.

If you own a microwave oven or have access to one, you can count on drying your roses in a few minutes. A regular gas or electric oven will take up to twelve hours, and heat the kitchen. A container standing in a dry place should take a couple of days, possibly three. Length of time depends on size of bloom, number of blooms being dried at once, even outdoor weather conditions. Start a collection of one pound coffee tins that come complete with plastic tight-fitting tops. For storage you can use cottage cheese or yogurt containers with tops. If these latter are not always a tight seal, improvise sealing with plastic cooking wrap, or sealing tape, which works. For ceramic covered dishes, ditto.

A glass, ceramic, or sturdy plastic container is required for a microwave oven; metal, ceramic, or tempered glass for a regular or electric toaster oven. To get ready, have the bottom third of the container, which should be not too much larger than the cut bloom, filled with silica gel.

For best results, cut a miniature rose, or roses, that is not too far open, that is dry and in good condition. Late morning or early afternoon of a bright day is a good time for cutting. However, if there's a wet rose out there asking to be cut, bring it in out of the rain and roll the bloom gently over a cushion of paper towels, or oft washed terry cloth that won't leave any lint. Avoid refrigeration. Roses dry more successfully when freshly cut.

Roses can change shade and sometimes hue with drying, so don't depend on your knowledge or memory for names. Label your roses, and identify them by color, and if you're putting two or more into a container, place those of a different color in the same container. Then you can tape a note on the outside: name of rose, red blend. While you're at it, include the date.

If you're careful, you can use the rose stem and not cut it off; although many people like to gently force a wire through the rose receptacle, or calyx, using the wire as a stem. This is the generally recommended procedure, but try not removing the rose's stem. By working carefully you will be rewarded with the rose's own stem, plus its leaves, something a wire cannot produce. Many arrangers prefer it this way. A caveat, dry more than you think you will need, so if there are accidents along the way, or you change plans, you are protected.

Collect roses at different stages of openness to add interest to your arrangements and bouquets. It will be more demanding preparing the different stages, applying the silica gel to a fully open bloom, but as usual, the risks being greater, so are the rewards.

Place the rose, bloom up, in the container, at a slight slant so you can keep an eye on the leaves. Carefully insert stem end into the silica gel. Several tight buds may be laid side by side, at a large slant, leaflets as flat as possible; otherwise keep to one rose per container for best processing. For good control of the tiny blue grains, use a teaspoon for pouring. Gently add silica gel, letting it slide down sides of container until rose is supported, then sprinkle until the bloom is completely covered. Add crystals carefully into spaces between petals, possibly using your fingers for this most tricky phase. To move crystals about, especially around delicate petals, use a soft small brush. A camel's hair paintbrush is most often used. Add extra crystals. There is a risk of mildew if the rose is not completely dry.

If you elect to cut off stems you might fit several blooms into the container for drying. Put wire through calyx and twist ends into a ponytail with enough length to manipulate, either for adding a wood stem (pic) or another length of wire. One advantage to using wire stem is that it is easier to adjust length for an arrangement or display. Or you can leave a tiny piece of toothpick in the calyx, enough to glue on to, or to remove and insert a pic, a stem from another flower, or a wire. A wired bloom may not be safe from fire in a microwave oven, and should be dried either in a conventional oven or standing safely in a corner.

Using a microwave oven, do not cover container, though some people do. For other methods, seal tightly. Heat in microwave one or two minutes. Because of differences in size and heat control of microwave ovens, you will need to become familiar with the one you're using. Important: put a glass of water into a corner of the microwave oven for heating period. In a regular gas or electric oven, heat at 150 or 200 degrees. For standard drying, place tightly covered container in a room of average temperature away from drafts, in driest possible corner.

At proper time, depending on medium you have used, test for readiness by pouring off a bit of the gel, and if petals are not totally dry, replace gel slowly as before and test again, a minute for microwave, or hours later for regular ovens. Petal tips should look and, touching gently, feel paper-y. If not, replace seal tightly, except for microwave oven, and let process continue.

After removal from oven, let container stand to cool and set. If petals feel taffy-like and do not flop, they should be thoroughly dry and you can pour off crystals, gently, as you applied them. Rotate container slowly. With practice, just a look will tell you when roses are ready. Use small nylon or camel's hair brush to remove stubborn crystals. Have ready a box lined with a layer of silica gel covered with tissue paper; place roses lightly onto tissue, not touching any part of each other. Store in covered box. For your own use, and for longer preservation, you might want to spray a light coat of sealer over specimens, but not for show competition where it is illegal and would cost you points. The sealer used by

Secrets of the Miniature Rose

artists for their charcoal drawings is lightest and does not provide too much shine.

If you've experimented with stemmed specimens, stand them in containers with a bit of silica gel at bottom, complete with labeled name and dates, ready for use.

Although silica gel is expensive initially, it can be reused almost indefinitely. As it absorbs moisture from the flowers the blue crystals lose their color, and you can tell when it is no longer effective. Next, it is time for drying the gel itself. Spread crystals over a baking pan, heat in a barely warm, at 225, conventional gas or electric oven until the flowers return to their original blue coloring. By alternating batches of gel, you'll always have some on hand in condition for use.

All the modern methods are efficient but none so nostalgic as pressing. Victorian lovers pressed flowers of sweet memory into pages of a novel, or the family Bible, or family history. Pages and ages have yellowed, paper for photograph albums is now of more lasting quality, and even sentiments have changed, but a single rose still has heartfelt value, can be pressed under the weight of any flat surface, between two paper towels or two sheets of white paper, weighted down, or, following tradition, between pages of a special book. Not sophisticated nor professional, simply tender and romantic.

A chancy, homey, method of drying is just letting the flowers dry. Enjoy an arrangement, don't add water after a few days. See if the roses dry to an almost perfect color without changing condition. This is unorthodox, but it has worked. It has been successful with miniature roses and other plant materials whether they've been in oasis or on a needlepoint holder, so long as you start out with a container properly filled with water and rose(s) properly conditioned.

A commonly used method is hanging plant materials upside down to dry like laundry on a clothesline, only in a dark space tied to a coat hanger, but for some reason this is not wholly successful with roses. It is certainly worth a try especially because it is so easy, but be sure not to cut off air circulation. Freeze drying is another method that works beautifully, and time on the machine can be ordered from some florists. It is very expensive but with wedding bouquets and other flower arrangements of significance, it is worth whatever the charge.

Lighter colored petals seem to retain their original color more surely than red, which means you should either dry more red roses to have greater numbers of successful drieds, or plan on making more designs and bouquets with lighter colored roses. It's always practical to have extra dried specimens to choose from, especially if you change your design as you proceed, or if a certain specimen proves inadequate. Handled delicately, dried miniature roses can be ordered into gracious permanent bouquets, wreaths, and designs, at home everywhere.

Miniature Directions

1. Collect roses at their driest, noon or early afternoon; if damp, roll dry on paper towel or terry cloth.

2. Stand rose at slight slant in appropriate container partly filled with silica gel. Drip gel gently into flowers and around foliage until specimen is fully covered.

3. Experiment with covering tightly or not for microwave use.

4. Place glass of water in corner.

5. Identify roses in containers.

6. Peek after proper time for drying process. Test.

7. Remove when specimen is completely dry.

Secrets of the Miniature Rose

8. Store in covered container, with small amount of silica gel.

9. Experiment with simply allowing roses to dry.

10. Try hanging roses upside down in dark corner to dry.

10e: Beauty by Arrangement

A BLOOM among its peers in a miniature rose bed has a different impact on us humans when gathered and removed to an arrangement. A beautiful rose can look even more alluring in a beautiful arrangement.

You can sit all day in your garden and watch the bushes grow, or you can take a table out there and work surrounded by lovely miniature roses in bloom, but you can't do it all the time, and if you have plants in a window box, or under lights, or in pots at the front entrance, you can't do your desk work, entertain there, or decorate the hall table. Therefore you make an arrangement for yourself, for a dinner party, for a friend—or perhaps for an exhibition in a show.

A certain style goes with flower arranging, and so does a cache of properties such as containers and mechanical aids, but more than that, a backup of home grown flowers to choose from. A single bush can produce enough blooms to supply two or more arrangements, and it's a good place to start. There's always time to add to your flower supply.

Arranging miniroses in an attractive design is a spin-off activity of rose growing that crosses age and gender lines, and is increasing in popularity each year. You can grow other flowers and line material to include in your arrangements, find suitable materials on a pleasant walk in the country, or buy them at a local florist's. Small branches of nearby trees or bushes can be cut to size, or your own minirose bushes can spare a branch here and there to fill in as line material. Give weeds a second look as you pick them They may constitute a nuisance in the garden, but some are truly attractive in an arrangement.

Building a collection of containers adds spice to the venture. It is surprising what lends itself: covers of lipstick cases, seashells, salt cellars minus their tops, dollhouse teapots, homemade containers out of film cases, demitasse cups— just about anything that is appropriate for the type of arrangement you intend it for.

Abstract arrangements use plant materials differently from the way in which they grow, have more than one center of interest, use open space as an important part of the design. Modern arrangements use plant and other materials in exciting new ways and have no traditional patterns. Their main characteristics are boldness in color and form, dynamic lines, textural contrast. Mass arrangements have depth, are outlined by reaching flowers, grouped in a geometric shape, oval or triangle or sphere. Line designs emphasize their line of beauty, have little depth except for their center of interest, have good rhythmic movement, as have all successful arrangements.

Colors take on an importance as center of interest or accent, contributing to rhythm and focus. Try different color backgrounds to enhance a deep pink or lavender rose; place the container on a base, for grace, for stability, for height. Spare designs emphasizing line require fewer roses, less plant material, but can have strong appeal. It is the use of space that establishes the quality of a design. Some designs combine line emphasis with mass interest, a line-mass arrangement. However you choose, plan before you begin.

Some people find the art of flower arranging as much a part of their lives as music or reading. Read one or more of the innumerable good books on flower arranging that have been and are being published. Haunt your local library and bookstore. Understand the principles of design: balance, proportion, scale, dominance, contrast, and all-important rhythm. Know the elements within your control and see them as contributing to the good looks of what you do: line, form, pattern, texture, size, space, and beautiful color. Books, except for some ARS books, don't usually have chapters on miniature arrangements and will hardly refer to miniature roses, but all design elements, principles, and other guidelines apply to any and all arrangements.

Become familiar with American Rose Society's *Guidelines for Judging Rose Arrangements.* There you will find descriptions of different types of arrangements, and helpful illustrations.

To begin, take stock of what you have to work with: roses, other plant materials, containers, small needlepoint holders, floral foam, and mechanics such as tape, fine wire, a glue gun for putting small things together. Perishables need the most attention. Rules for gathering roses are always, except for drying, the same: Late afternoon or early morning take a pail of cool water to the garden, cut stems longer than needed, recut under water; let roses stand in water almost up to the bloom. Place pail in a cool dark situation and let roses stand till water cools, then place roses in refrigerator to harden overnight or for at least two hours, if possible, before arranging.

Many professional arrangers have made public in books or lectures their special methods for prolonging the life of their flowers. Here are some you can try, to determine for yourself which you prefer. The main fact is that a rose cared for properly in the garden since it was planted will last in the design, and even the better part of a day out of water. Once cut, subsequent treatment, no matter how detailed, cannot make up for negligence or poor care in the garden.

Using a commercial flower preservative together with a small amount of bleach (1/2 tsp. per quart) can add days to the life of an arrangement. So will changing the water every two or three days, especially if you follow a ritual procedure: Place the arrangement into a temporary container filled with standing water, wash the permanent container, refill with preservative-sweetened standing water, and replace arrangement. If there is enough stem, you can cut stem tips under water before replacing, but usually this is not practicable because it can mean doing over the entire design.

The following method is a little more effort, but your roses represent effort and monetary investment, which justifies the extras. Into a cup of standing water, stir a half teaspoon of alcohol and a half teaspoon of peppermint oil. Before roses are refrigerated, stems are dipped about a half to one inch into the peppermint oil solution for two or three minutes, then replaced into cool water and into the refrigerator. This is a formidable method for maintaining freshness of designs.

Another possibility is to dip the tips of canes into an inch of rather hot faucet water, prior to refrigeration. This requires a narrow-necked container into which to dip the stem end, or the bloom and nearby foliage can be protected by a shield so the water vapor does not reach foliage and bloom.

A dry wrapped rose can be treated by one of these methods after it has been unwrapped and revived—but remember to consider all the angles before plunging into something new. So, try any, all, or none, of these methods. They're the equivalent of grandmother's recipes. The first one, most simple, is a good place to begin, and should work for you.

And what works on the show table will work at home. If you want to design an arrangement for your own use and not be bound by schedule and show rules, you are limited only by facilities at your command. A hurry-up line arrangement can be assembled in a flash if you take three stems of the same variety, or, at least, hue: one a color-showing bud, the longest; the second a partly open bloom; and the third a

1

2

1 Abstract Arrangement by
   Steven House
   TERRY ELLIS

2 Mass Arrangement by
   Steven House
   TERRY ELLIS

3 All Miniature Rose Show
   RANDY LADY

4 Table Arrangement
   RANDY LADY

3

4

1

2

3

1 English Box
LARRY BUSTER

2 English Box
RANDY LADY

3 Mass Arrangement
RANDY LADY

4 Artist's Palette
GEORGE MANDER

❧

4

1

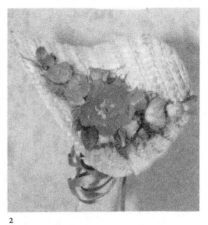

2

3

1 Rose in a Bowl
LARRY BUSTER

2 Rosecraft (hat, dried)
RANDY LADY

3 Keepsake (dried)
TONY BARBARO

4 Wreath (dried)
TONY BARBARO

4

3

1

2

4

1 Mass Arrangement
RANDY LADY

2 Hogarth Curve
E. ABLER

3 Mass Arrangement (dried)
RANDY LADY

4 Oriental Manner Moribana
TERRY ELLIS

1

2

3

4

1

2

3

4

Three-Inch Arrangements

1 Mass Arrangement - Coral Bells
RICH BAER

2 Mass Arrangement - Spice Drop
RICH BAER

3 Japanese Manner Arrangement -
Little Megan
RICH BAER

4 Line Arrangement -
Baby Betsy McCall
RICH BAER

෯

1 8-inch Arrangement (dried)
BEVERLY PARRISH

2 Oriental Manner Free Style
RANDY LADY

3 Modern Free Form
RANDY LADY

4 Rosecraft (dried)
RANDY LADY

1

2

3

4

1 Mass Arrangement by
Steven House
TERRY ELLIS

2 Line Mass Arrangement
RANDY LADY

3 Abstract Arrangement by
Steven House
TERRY ELLIS

bloom at exhibition stage. Wire them inconspicuously together in that order, one just beneath the other, and cut the stems with one cut. Place in a suitable container with a taller twig or branch for line material and interest, or with no extra line material if you like. Presto, a lovely line arrangement.

Three-inch arrangements can seem most difficult because everything is so exaggeratedly small. Three inches means overall, cubically, but even so, the blooms must be proportionate to the size of the design, which includes the container. Micro minis and some of the smaller varieties suit this requirement well, but for practice, consider not measuring exactly to any particular size until you feel comfortable working in small measurements. Then cut a three-inch square of cardboard for use as a measuring guide as you form your arrangement.

The current love affair with Japanese flower arranging, ikebana, is no passing fancy. Around the world there are study groups lead by native Japanese teachers, or by people who have studied in Japan. The influence, started around the beginning of the twentieth century, has reached across continents and into the hearts of countrymen everywhere. Ideas have been sent both ways. European and American flowers are being used by Japanese. European and American ideas are being integrated into flower arranging by the Japanese, and the evidence is clear that the Japanese have influenced our way of arranging flowers. Simplicity and strength of line, together with the importance of controlling space, now influence flower arrangers in all parts of the world.

Students are taught the importance and significance of the scalene triangle, but jiyuka, or free style, now pervades the creativity of the Japanese ikebana professors who love to do free arranging—after years of studying and mastering the rules, techniques, and symbolism of moribana, nageire, shoka, and rikka, the traditional forms.

Living with Miniatures

It's reverence for nature that drives the traditional Japanese arrangement. The wonderful rikka, formulated hundreds of years ago, represents a landscape. Then came shoka, in the late 1600s, simpler to do, but elegant, too, emphasizing natural life with its three lines forming a triangle: shin (truth), soe, and tai. Moribana and nageire came later but retain the asymmetrical form, and the feeling for nature.

Small arrangements interpret the Japanese schools of flower arrangement delightfully. If you copy some of the simpler designs from one of the fascinating books available, you'll soon be an adherent.

Early American arrangements were essentially bouquets, copied from European flower designers. Until women banded together in flower or garden clubs, there were no special design types. Love of flowers, however, seems to transcend distance and diverse cultures.

Don't let it bother you if your first small arrangements aren't the greatest thing since hybridizing. As you think of ways to put different materials together, and keep your eyes peeled for interesting containers, you'll be experimenting in your mind's eye and at the work table. Sometimes combining other flowers may enrich your design, so stay with it. When you visit any exhibit or a rose show, imagine how you would do this or that design. Imagine how any flower arrangement would look with your roses.

Take your camera with you, snap the designs you like, large or small. You can often translate a standard size design into a small one. If there's a schedule available, take it home and do the miniature classes with your own roses, using materials and containers at hand. Since miniature arrangements range up to ten inches cubically, you have plenty of variety to work with.

In spite of yourself, it happens over and over again. You get started, and can't stop. Your mind turns to seeing roses in a design, and then in competition in a show. When this happens to you, be prepared. To insure having an adequate selection for a planned design, plant at least two bushes of each variety you prefer, micro minis and larger varieties, of your favorite colors.

ARS shows are planned for peak bloom in the area where local, district, or national shows are staged, especially because rules require that all roses be outdoor garden grown. Garden club rules differ from ARS rules, as plant material may be florist bought, and other differences. Some garden club shows have a Petite award for eight-or-less inch arrangements, which does not require any specific kind of flower and where miniature roses would walk right in. Other garden club shows have eight- or nine-inch niches of a specified color background, gray or white, etc., and ask for particular designs to grace them. Many schedules have classes for dried arrangements, permitting you to use your own flowers out of season.

Chapter 11 has sample show schedules and judging information for reference. You will be better able to plan your arrangements and choose varieties for your garden if you know what to expect.

Maybe you don't want to compete at all, or only sometimes; then place your design as a centerpiece on a breakfast or dinner table, a living room cocktail table, on an office desk, a hospital lunch tray, a bedroom dresser, or nestled in a wall-hung container. It's all for pleasure, and you can start any time—such as right now.

Miniature Directions

1. Become familiar with design principles and elements. Read books on design available in books stores and garden sections of public libraries. Be familiar with ARS *Guidelines for Judging Rose Arrangements*.

Living with Miniatures

2. In the garden and/or under lights, cultivate a repertoire of miniature roses for arrangements.

3. Have fun collecting containers.

4. Make arrangements for yourself, for friends, for exhibition using fresh or dried miniroses.

CHAPTER 11

Exhibit Your Roses

VIRTUALLY ANY flower show anywhere will welcome rose exhibitors in either horticulture or artistic design sections, with the exception of specialty flower shows, e.g., dahlia, iris, orchid, etc. Opportunities are many and beckoning. There are garden clubs and rose societies in every state of the Union, and in countries around the world.

American Rose Society members eagerly hold rose shows in their various local branches at least once a year. The objective is to provide a forum for exhibiting roses at peak of bloom, to foster enthusiasm for rose growing, and to educate and encourage the public to participate.

Rules for entering an exhibit are usually clear and precise, aimed at avoiding disagreements, and ultimately, disappointments. In most garden clubs and flower societies show rules are an evolving proposition. Superimposed on a scorecard specifying points for what is being judged, judging is considered an art, so differences of opinion are unavoidable, but most judges, exhibitors, and viewers agree in the main. And so the shows go on.

Garden clubs hold regular flower shows and rarely have classes strictly for miniature roses, but unless they limit or designate the kind of flower permitted, there is no reason you cannot enter an arrangement incorporating miniroses in the design classes, a specimen in the horticulture division, or a bush in the houseplant section. Some garden club rules consider miniature arrangements as five-inch designs; ARS considers the term "miniature arrangements" to designate arrangements using miniature roses, and limits miniature arrangements to ten inches.

Here are some sample sections from rose society and garden club schedules to help you become acquainted with what is expected and permitted, and to familiarize you with rules for participating in shows.

Some general rules, abridged here, for exhibiting specimens in a rose show: (because ARS judging is evolutionary, updated rules are announced from time to time.)

1. Entries will be received from 7 A.M. to 10 A.M. Judging will begin at 10:15 A.M. Exhibitors tags and containers will be provided. Both top and bottom sections of the entry tag must be filled in.

2. All entries in horticulture classes must have been grown in the exhibitor's own garden.

3. Rules of the American Rose Society for exhibiting and judging, and rules governing disqualification, will be strictly observed, such as the following: when a specimen is misspelled; misnamed; mislabeled or unlabeled; misclassed; stem on stem; when there's presence of a foreign substance applied to foliage, stem, or bloom to improve the appearance of the specimen; when there is a side bud or buds on a specimen that must be shown disbudded; when a specimen is in violation of ARS rules or local society rules; when a specimen is not registered with ARS; when the appearance of the exhibitor's name is in any location other than designated places on the entry tag.

4. Aluminum foil is the only wedging material permitted to position a specimen in its container. (This rule may vary around the country.)

5. Trophies and certificates will go to blue ribbon winners only.

ARS Scale of points for evaluating specimens:

Form 25 points	Stem & Foliage 20 points
Color 20 points	Size 10 points
Substance 15 points	Balance and Proportion 10 points

Some challenge classes for miniature roses:

1. Six miniature roses, no more than two of a variety, exhibited in an English box. Foliage permitted, not necessary. Boxes available by reservation.

2. Six miniature roses exhibited in an English box. All the same variety. Foliage not permitted.

3. One miniature rose in an open bowl, to be judged for quality of bloom and appropriateness to bowl. Foliage permitted. Bowl to be furnished by exhibitor.

4. Three miniature sprays, all different varieties, in exhibition form. Exhibited in separate containers.

Examples of specimen class requirements:

1. Miniatures, one bloom per stem, no side buds; must be disbudded. Entries eligible for Miniature Queen, King, Princess, and Prince.

2. Miniatures. One spray; more than one bloom per stem; unwanted growth may be removed.

3. Open bloom miniatures. One bloom per stem. Stamens must show.

Exhibit Your Roses

Rules for Artistic Design classes nominally include rules above, plus rules specifically for arrangements. Herewith sample arrangement rules in abridged form:

1. All classes and trophies are open to members of the American Rose Society or a local rose society.

2. One entry per class permitted. Names of varieties must appear on entry tag. A card of intent is desirable but not required.

3. A rose or roses must provide the dominant flower interest. All roses must be outdoor garden grown and of good quality.

4. Other flowers, foliage, dried, and/or treated materials, and accessories permitted, but not necessary.

5. There are but two causes for disqualification: Roses not outdoor garden grown, and use of artificial plant material. Other rule infringements will result in penalty.

6. The Miniature Royalty, Oriental, Court of Etiquette, and Artist's Awards will go to eligible blue ribbon winners scoring 92 points or more.

7. Miniature arrangements may be ten inches or less. Designs need not be size limit specified in class descriptions, but are penalized for exceeding limit.

8. Gold, silver, and Bronze certificates will be awarded to top three worthy blue ribbon arrangements scoring 92 points or more, if roses are arranger-grown (AG), and it is so noted on entry tag.

ARS Scorecard for judging all rose arrangements:

Conformance	20 points
Design (5 points per principle)	30 points
Perfection of the rose(s) and other plant material	30 points
Creativity and Expressiveness	10 points
Distinction	10 points

Classes that would be eligible for the Miniature Royalty Award:

1. A Valentine party. Line arrangement. Red, white, and red blend roses only. Not to exceed seven inches in height, width, or depth.

2. Sleeping Beauty. Line-mass arrangement. Not to exceed nine inches in height, width, or depth.

3. Circus World. Mass arrangement. Design not to exceed four inches in height, width, or depth.

The following classes would be eligible for the Miniature Artist's Award:

1. Computer Fancy. Free Form. Design not to exceed ten inches in height, width, or depth.

2. It Takes Two to Tango (or polka, waltz, or fox trot, etc.) Design using two containers, not to exceed seven inches in height, width, or depth.

3. Astrologer. Any sign of the Zodiac. A five-inch modern (free form or abstract) arrangement. Sign and type of design to be named on tag.

The following classes would be eligible for the Miniature Oriental Award:

1. Kyoto on My Mind. Design in the oriental manner, not to exceed eight inches in height, width, or depth. Moribana. (low container)

2. Oh, Fujiama. Design in the Oriental manner, not to exceed nine inches in height, width, or depth. Nageire. (tall container)

Horticulture rules may vary with the two major national garden clubs in this country. In general, because there is variety of horticulture that does not apply to rose societies, naming of entries should include botanical name, genus, and species, etc., and length of time entries must have been in possession of exhibitor.

Examples of classes from various shows:

> *From a GCA club: Hanging Containers: flowering or fruiting plant(s); container 6" or under. Arrangements: Small niche: Framed opening, 12" high x 10" wide, interior floor, 9 ³/₄" wide x 7" deep.*

1. Crown Jewels. A composition. No jewelry permitted.

2. Import-Export. A design incorporating an import.

3. Win or Lose. An interpretation of a game; to be named.

> *Miniature Dried arrangements, not to exceed 5" in any direction.*

1. Tranquility "Ever Let the Fancy Roam," John Keats. A design of dried plant material.

2. A design of dried plant material in the oriental mood.

3. VCR. A design very clearly red.

> *From a local garden club offering the Federated Petite Award:*

1. Going to Sea. Eligible for the Petite Award. A small design of fresh and/or dried plant material, no more than eight inches in any dimension. A horizontal design.

> *From a local garden club: Enchanted Time:*

1. October's Last Blooms. A small design using all fresh plant material not to exceed 8" in any dimension.

Secrets of the Miniature Rose

2. Mementos of Autumn. A miniature design using all dried plant material, not to exceed 5" in any dimension.

From another garden club:

1. Light As A Feather. A small design using all dried plant material. To be placed in a niche 9" high, 9" wide, 9" deep.

2. Fledglings. A miniature design not to exceed 3" in any direction using all fresh plant material. To be placed in a circular (4" diameter) lighted niche.

Note: If you read through the section on Beauty by Arrangement, Chapter 10e, and use this section as a guide and jumping off place, you will be familiar with all the procedures of a formal or informal show, and prepared to be no more nervous than any veteran exhibitor.

CHAPTER 12

Aboard the
ARS

❧

N EWCOMERS TO roses think the American Rose Society (ARS) is somewhere out there, and, indeed, it is. Not until they have visited a local society meeting, listened to the absorbed speakers, and met the equally absorbed-in-roses members, do newcomers realize that joining is for them, too.

It's not required, nor even necessary, and probably not for everyone, but ARS is a supportive, informative, searching, and interested group of people from most levels of American life—bound together by love of roses. The member you meet may be a computer programmer, a nurse, mail carrier, teacher, steamfitter, thoracic surgeon, a chemist.

Approximately 21,000 rosarians eagerly await the monthly ARS news-filled magazine bringing articles written by experienced exhibitors, growers, researchers, hybridizers, merchandisers, scientists. Fascinating reports on new roses together with tempting photos, opinions on value of varieties, society shows, national conventions, newly developed spray materials, cultural practices; and a plenitude of rose related reporting. Since 1981 the ARS is legally certified a 501(c)(3) education organization, and therefore certain expenses connected with society participation are deductible for income tax purposes

The Society is structured so that every member from anywhere in the United States is an active participant. Two Board approved national conventions a year, rotating in location around the country, provide abundant opportunity for exchange of information, viewing and showing roses, maintenance of acquaintance and friendship, and forum for learning. Conventions are normally scheduled by the host society at peak time of local area rose bloom, both spring and fall, where a national show of roses in horticulture and design is the first order of business. Competition is keen, and rewards are commensurate with magnitude of difficulty: satisfaction, beauty, high honor, ribbons, trophies, and card certificates with gold, silver, and bronze shields.

Since 1999, and growing in popularity, an all-miniature once-a-year national show and conference has taken the fancy of rosarians. Same as for national conventions, local societies apply to the Board for permission to host the customary meeting. Programs are offered, similar to those at national conventions, but are confined to subjects directly applicable to miniatures.

ARS extends its hand to every member. States are grouped into weather and area-related districts, each of which have their own director, meetings, and activities. Members journey long hours and miles to attend a district convention, exhibit their roses in the attendant show. Local societies work within district coordination, usually meet once a month, and maintain constant contact with members by publishing a bulletin containing articles on aspects of rose growing and news of society activities.

Local societies mount their own annual shows, plan monthly programs designed to stimulate the old-timers, and instruct newcomers. Probably the most popular of these is the customary annual garden walk at which rosarians open their gardens to fellow members. It's a plenitude of roses and rose information. The moment something new or different comes to light, it is written about in ARS magazine and society bulletin. New roses are tried in the garden, discussed from every point of view. You can participate as much or as little as you choose. Numbers of members are so enthusiastic they belong to several local societies because of friendships, contacts, news bulletins, interesting programs.

A significant and ever-growing arm of the ARS is support of research and advancement of the rose, maintenance of test gardens, scheduling college level seminars. One major ARS project is planting and maintenance of the various sections of extensive gardens at ARS headquarters in Shreveport, Louisiana. The gardens are a tourist attraction, open free to all members, are available for rental for weddings, meetings, and social events. Newer and older varieties are displayed in grand design, tended by experts: old garden roses, floribundas, grandifloras, hybrid teas, stately tree roses, climbers—and miniatures of all sizes.

A viable system for training and accrediting rose horticulture and arrangement judges is constantly updated. Judges take their responsibilities seriously, polish their skills, travel hours to judge a show—and lunch with fellow judges and local society friends.

Every three years there is a meeting of national rose societies in countries around the world: Canada, England, Australia, Germany, France. In 1974, the World Federation convened in the United States. These meetings, open to all members, provide information exchange, international cooperation, exciting travel experiences.

Other important advantages to ARS membership include book borrowing privileges by mail; access to rigorously trained consulting rosarians around the United States who are dedicated ARS advisors, access to Roses in Review, the annual reassessment of ratings of individual roses for garden and exhibition quality; access to the American Rose Annual, a volume of high quality articles of rose interest accompanied by comparable photographs. A paid and competent staff runs the office, edits publications, and is helpful to members.

One outstanding achievement of the ARS is the sponsorship of the rose as America's national flower, or, technically, floral emblem of the United States. President Ronald Reagan signed the proclamation on November 20, 1986. The rewards will continue, and everyone can participate. For membership information, contact:

> American Rose Society-A
> P.O. Box 30,000
> Shreveport, Louisiana 71130-0030
> Phone: 318-938-5402

AMERICAN BOX   See "English box."

ARS   American Rose Society

APICAL BUD   The first formed bud in a cluster, usually the largest; or, the bud nearest or at the top of the bush.

APICAL DOMINANCE   The nature of rose bushes to develop buds and blooms from the top down.

AXIL   The angle formed by a cane and the leaf or lateral growing from it.

AXILLARY BUD   The bud formed within an axil.

BALLING   Petals of a bloom hug each other and form a ball.

BLIND SHOOT   A cane, or shoot, which does not produce a bud.

BUD EYE   The incipient bud within an axil.

CACHEPOT   A decorative container to hold and disguise a utility pot.

CALYX   The sepals of a flower, forming a protective receptacle.

CANDELABRA   A dispropor-tionately large cane, usually developing directly from the roots with at least one, if not several, clusters of buds and bloom at the top or tip.

CLIMBER   A miniature rose bush producing canes that reach from five to eight or more feet, yet having no tendrils for clinging.

CONVENIENCE CAN   A spray can ready for use, containing fungicides and insecticide in proper proportion, purchasable where garden supplies are sold. Spray materials vs. blackspot, mildew, rust, insects—sometimes including a miticide.

DEADHEADING   Removing spent or dying blooms from a bush.

DIEBACK   The dying, blackening of a left-over cane or canes after bush has been pruned.

DISBUD   To remove from a stem a bud or buds while still tender, leaving only the apical bud; in a spray the apical bud is removed.

DRIP LINE An imaginary circle formed on the ground just underneath the reach of the leaves of a bush, where water may drip.

ENGLISH BOX In ARS shows, a rectangular and covered box with a specified number of openings (usually six) for inserting blooms. Canes are cut long enough to reach the concealed tubes holding water. An American box may have nine or twelve openings.

FLORIFEROUS Bearing, or capable of bearing, many blooms.

FRIABLE SOIL Tillable, easily handled soil.

FULL BLOWN A fully open bloom, stamens showing. Not applicable to a single.

GRADE Ground level.

GUTTATION Water exuding from specialized pores at leaflet edges.

HARDEN To condition plant material.

HIPS The colorful seed pods of a rose bush. The mature ovary.

HUMUS Decomposed, stable organic matter.

IKEBANA Japanese word for flower arranging.

IKENOBO Oldest and largest school of Japanese flower arranging.

INTERNODE The distance between two nodes.

LATERAL A branch or cane growing from a primary cane.

LEAF BURN See "spray burn."

LIVE EYE A bud eye that shows pink, or some evidence of life.

MICRO-CLIMATE An area within any location where weather is different from surroundings.

MULCH A protective covering applied to the soil surface.

MUTATION A chance change in a gene that produces offspring different from what is expected.

NODE The point at which a leaf or branch emerges from a stem or cane.

PAINT To protect a cut or wound by covering it with a sealing agent.

PEDUNCLE Neck of the bloom. That section at the top of a stem above the foliage.

PETIOLE Stem or stalk, the neck, of a leaf.

PETIOLULE Stem or stalk of a leaflet.

pH The relative value of acidity and alkalinity in soil or a solution. pH means: "potential of hydrogen."

PHOTOSYNTHESIS Plants manufacturing their (and our) food by converting light energy to chemical energy.

PISTIL The flower organ consisting of ovary, style, and stigma.

PITH The central tissue within the bark of a cane.

PRIMARY CANE A cane growing directly from the roots, or from an axil.

ROOT BALL See "soil ball."

133

Appendix I: Glossary

SCALENE TRIANGLE   A triangle having three unequal sides.

SHATTER   When petals drop randomly from a full blown bloom.

SHOVEL PRUNE   v.t. To dig up.

SINGLE   A rose with from five to twelve petals, usually five, with petals radiating from a center of stamens.

SOIL BALL   The roots, and soil, clinging to and protecting the roots. Sometimes called the root ball.

SPORT   A surprise genetic change that produces a bloom different from the host.

SPRAY BURN   Brown, dry edges of leaves, some dark spots on leaves.

STANDING WATER   Water that has been drawn and stored in an uncovered pitcher or like container for four hours or more, preferably overnight.

STEM-ON-STEM   A situation where a stem or branch is not independent, but includes a part of the stem from which it originated.

STOMA   A minute pore occurring in large numbers on underside of leaflets, and in lesser numbers on surfaces, which permits passage of gasses and water vapor. Plural: stomata.

TEETH   Indentations on leaflet margins of many miniature rose varieties, forming sharp outlines faintly resembling teeth.

TISSUE CULTURE   Method of propagating many exact reproductions of a plant from selected small parts, cultivated in a special substance in a controlled environment.

TLC   Commonly used shorthand for "tender loving care."

TURGID   Full. Having substance. A plant cell is turgid when it is full with water, and firm.

VEGETATIVE CENTERS, OR GROWTH   Bloom centers that are imperfectly formed, or without proper petals, or having short petals, or no petals. Vegetative growth in foliage is excessive foliage production without buds, or sparse budding.

WATER WAND   A hose attachment that forcefully directs water.

APPENDIX II: ON LOCATION

Healthy roses and good service may be expected from the following nurseries that advertise in the *American Rose* magazine:

Bridges Roses
2734 Toney Road
Lawndale, NC 28090
704-538-9412

Sequoia Nursery
Moore Miniature Roses
2519 E. Noble Ave.
Visalia, CA 93292
559-732-0309

Nor'East Miniature
Roses
P.O. Box A
Rowley, MA 01969
800-426-6485

Tiny Petals Nursery
2880 Ramsey Cutoff
Silver Springs, NV
89429
775-577-4474

Taylor's Roses,
P.O. Box 677
Fairhope, AL 36533
251-928-5008

Kimbrew-Walter Roses
2001 VZ County Rd
1219
Grand Saline, TX
75140-4755
877-597-6737

Michigan Mini Roses
45951 Hull Road
Belleville, MI 48111
734-699-6698

Justice Miniature Roses
SW Kahle Road 5947
Wilsonville, OR 97070
503-682-2370

Jackson & Perkins
Company
One Rose Lane
Medford, OR 97501
800-292-4769

Rosemania
4020 Trail Ridge Drive
Franklin, TN 37067
888-600-9665

Mitchie's Roses, 830 S.
373rd St, Federal Way,
WA 98003
253-815-1072

George Mander
2232 Gale Avenue
Coquitlam, BC
Canada V3K2YH
604-936-6661

INDEX

All-America Rose Selections, 5, 17
American Beauty, 3
American Rose Society (ARS), 4, 5, 89; and hybridizer, 104; arrangement scorecard, 124; color classes of, 17; evaluation scale of, 123; judging guidelines of, 115; overview of, 128–31; photography and, 101; show rules of, 88, 119, 121, 122–25; variety survey of, 17–18
anatomy, of rose, 9, 13
aphids, 58, 62, 63
apical bud, 90, 132
apical dominance, 12, 31, 132
arranging, 113–17; Japanese, 117–18; and photography, 118
axil, 31, 33, 92, 132
axillary bud, 132

Baby Katie, 102
balling, 132
beds, 23–24, 27, 28
black spot, 38, 41, 57, 58, 59, 60, 62, 63, 66–67, 84
blind shoot, 33, 34, 132

botrytis, 41, 57
burying bush, 55, 56, 69–71

cachepot, 53, 75, 132
calyx, 109, 110, 132
candelabra, 34, 132
Carolyn Dean, 4
cell, 8–9, 10
chlorophyll, 8, 9, 10
chlorosis, 45
climber, 16, 18–19, 35, 132
collar, 68
cone, 70, 71
convenience can, 54, 61, 132
Correvon, Henri, 3–4
Cutie, 4

deadheading, 32, 33, 132
dieback, 132
disbud, 41, 90, 93, 132
dormancy, 12, 24, 29, 43, 54–55, 66
drip line, 44, 50, 133
dry wrap, 93, 94, 116
drying, 107–13
dusting, 59

English box, 88, 133
ethylene, 12–13

Index

Index